TEACH ME TO PRAY

The No Fluff Christian User Guide to Overcome Doubt, Beat Distractions, and Develop a Meaningful Consistent Prayer Life — One Step at a Time

Mark Miller

First paperback edition December 2025

ISBN 979-8-9943401-0-3

Published by Inner Man Press
www.innermanpress.org

Does God really hear me?

Can I be sure God will answer?

Why is it difficult to maintain the habit of prayer?

Do I have enough faith to be heard?

What does it mean to pray in Jesus' name?

How can I know His will?

What is the "right" way to pray?

Does prayer help in overcoming sin?

How should I confess my sins?

How does the Spirit intercede for me?

Doesn't God already know it all anyway?

Is fasting still a thing?

Dear Reader,

This book didn't begin as a book at all—but with those questions.

My search for those answers became the framework for a series of lesson plans which I shared with several congregations. That material became a slide presentation, which in turn gave rise to a series of devotions published weekly from May through December of 2016.

Requests for a printed collection of those devotions resulted in a rough booklet that I released around 2020. Finally, that collection was edited and expanded through several iterations, and this is the result. It is the record of my personal attempt to demystify prayer and to establish the relationship with God that only prayer allows.

I hope this book will aid your understanding of and motivation to pray. May God bless your efforts.

Mark Miller
mark@innermanpress.org

And it came about that while He was praying in a certain place, after He had finished, one of His disciples said to Him, "Lord, teach us to pray" (Luke 11:1).

Dear Reader

How to use this book

Each devotion in this book is a meal by itself; I would not suggest devouring all thirty-one of them this afternoon. They are best digested at the rate of one a day over the course of a month or weekly in a small-group Bible study so that the concepts introduced can be absorbed and implemented. I have attempted to write without the "fluff" that I so despise in many of today's books, and I hope the result is something that satisfies. Scriptures cited are in bold font to make them more easily identified and referenced for further study.

Take advantage of the ***Reflection Questions*** at the end of each lesson. We absorb and retain information so much better when we actively participate in the learning process, and the reasons for this are twofold. Reflection forces you to notice things you wouldn't see with a passive reading, and more importantly, the questions are intended to help you to face the truths you've read. It's easy to nod, shrug, and agree in principle without taking ownership of application. Some questions are uncomfortable, and you may be tempted to skip past them—don't. Respond with an honest answer *in writing on paper* even if the truth is, "I don't know," or, "I'm not willing to face that right now." Later you can work your way through the material again when you're ready to accept those challenges.

Warning: I regularly employ the use of sarcasm. The international wink symbol ;) will be used throughout to warn the unguarded reader.

Contents

1: Take Courage

Lack of Prayer

I am convinced that most Christians (not you of course) don't pray often or at all. That is not to say they don't bow their heads reverently at the appropriate times on Sunday or, like Philistines, they eat their food unblessed. I mean *pray* in the sense of regular, personal, private conversation with God for its own sake—not as a prerequisite for something else.

I believe this to be true for three reasons. First, Christians admit to struggling with prayer. Second, they find it difficult when they attempt it. Third, I expect my own experience is not unique, for I have too often struggled to maintain the habit.

Already I have lost some of my readers. What more could possibly be said about prayer that should be but hasn't been already? Jesus did it; we should too. The Lord's Prayer before meals should take care of the majority of problems. If that doesn't work, try fasting. ;)

Wrong Approach

For many, their approach to prayer is to blame. They pray because they must. In their mind prayer is a cross to be borne in the knowledge that drudgery drives sin from the soul. Others consider prayer a healthy habit like brushing their teeth. You may not see the difference, but it can't hurt. Still others pray when there simply is no other option. When circumstances grow so dark that all they can do is pray—they do.

It is my hope that when you've finished with this book, none of those motives will describe your habit of prayer. Prayer does drive sin from the soul, and it is appropriate when times are dark, but those motives will not *keep* you praying. They might be sufficient to get the ball rolling, but we need a reason to pray that remains after the initial burst of need or novelty has subsided.

Problematic Nature

The greatest obstacle to persistent prayer is us. We are fleshly by nature, but prayer demands just the opposite. An exercise of faith, prayer requires a conviction of the unseen. It is here that Christians have done prayer perhaps its greatest disservice. The modern irrational approach to faith has stripped Christendom of confidence in its own prayers and has given its faith-less neighbors even less. Unable to objectively determine if their prayers are answered, many Christians are unmotivated to pray them and sadly resort to blind superstition in search of God's will —that frequently serves their own desires.

If this is you, take courage. Prayer is not an unsolvable enigma meant to test blind devotion. Rather, prayer is the most basic of all Christian interactions with God and the foundation of our relationship with Him. Prayer can be great—meaningful, peaceful, and effective. Together we will investigate the objections to prayer and their rational answers, better motives to pray, Biblical examples and instructions, and some how-to suggestions.

By the time you've finished this book—I promise—you won't look at prayer the same again.

Reflection Questions

- Prayer can seem mystifying. What question about prayer from the prologue list—if answered—would give you the most confidence/motivation to pray? ______________

  ____

  Why? ____

  ____

- If you were to rate the content, consistency, and personal fulfillment of your prayers over the past year with an impartial letter grade, what would it be? ______

- By the time you've completed this book, your hope is that grade will have risen to a(n) ______

- Why is it worth working through thirty more lessons to raise the quality of your prayer life to that grade?

  ____

  ____

2: Getting Started

Why We Pray

Tragedy, heartbreak, and fear can be the catalysts that move us to pray. A sudden burst of piety often results from trying circumstances, and the properly penitent look for a speedy resolution from a God with whom they have recently become reacquainted. Rarely do such motives produce long-term results. Crises pass. Loss, jail, and divorce can make someone religious for a season, but when the outcome is determined, there is little reason to continue.

If our habit of prayer is to last, it must have lasting motivation—the motive of relationship. Here's a quick test. Make a mental pie chart of your time spent in conversation—not with foreign tech support—but conversation for pleasure and familiarity. Who gets the biggest slice of your time? The time pie will be directly proportional to your relationships.

Prayer is the best measure of your relationship with the Father. Prophecy, casting out demons, and even miracles are no substitute. Those who rely on these alone will be disappointed to learn that their works did not produce relationship. **"I never knew you;"** says Jesus, **"depart from Me, you who practice lawlessness"** (Matthew 7:23).

Married to Prayer

To understand prayer better, marriage is invaluable as a teaching tool, for as in marriage, conversation is the one area that cannot effectively be feigned. Couples may go through the motions of responsibility and romance, but they can't fake relational conversation. The former—though good in their own right—cannot replace time spent sharing the joys, fears, cares, and aspirations that define us. Similarly, you can fake everything else about Christianity, but alone in your prayer closet, there is nothing to hide behind.

As in marriage, conversation in prayer is not a matter of greater volume. Neither the number of prayers prayed nor the decibels at which they are uttered will ensure we are heard.

My dear wife, Jen, would not be impressed if I dutifully repeated to her the same mindless conversation every day or shouted it from modern digital street corners. The Lord isn't impressed either. **"But you, when you pray, go into your inner room, and when you have shut your door, pray to your Father who is in secret, and your Father who sees in secret will repay you"** (Matthew 6:5–7). Personal. Private. Prayer.

Prioritizing Prayer

I considered using the last segment today to shame you into praying more—and more effectively—but guilt is not a lasting motivator. Instead I will offer one observation and one suggestion.

Observation: everyone has time to pray. I have the same twenty-four hours every day that you have. If I say, "I didn't have time," what I mean is, "Other pursuits were more important to me." We must make better excuses if they are to be believed by anyone besides ourselves. ;)

Suggestion: state the obvious. If you scrolled for two hours through funny videos but didn't pray, acknowledge the truth aloud (to yourself). "Funniest cat fails is more important to me than prayer." Or perhaps, "I would rather be annoyed by the trivial postings of semi-strangers than speak with God." If it sounds odd to hear it spoken aloud, remember actions speak louder. Commit with me to make the time.

Reflection Questions

- Using the left column, number these motives honestly in order of their influence on your efforts to pray.

____ ____ Doing the right thing

____ ____ Ritual/habit

____ ____ Desperation

____ ____ Relationship with God

____ ____ Desired blessing

____ ____ Others' expectations

____ ____ It's trending

- Switching only two items, use the right column to reorder the list closer to the way you'd like it to be.
- If you ranked the people you speak with by the quality and consistency of your conversations, who would be your top three?

1. ____

2. ____

3. ____

- If you ranked God on the same scale by the quality and consistency of your prayers, what number would He receive? _____
- Why is it easy to go through the motions of Christianity without pursuing the relationship available through prayer? ______________________________
- What is unique about prayer that might make it uncomfortable for you to practice? ______________

  ____
- State the obvious! Write the most absurd but true thing that has taken the place of your prayers. ____________

  ____

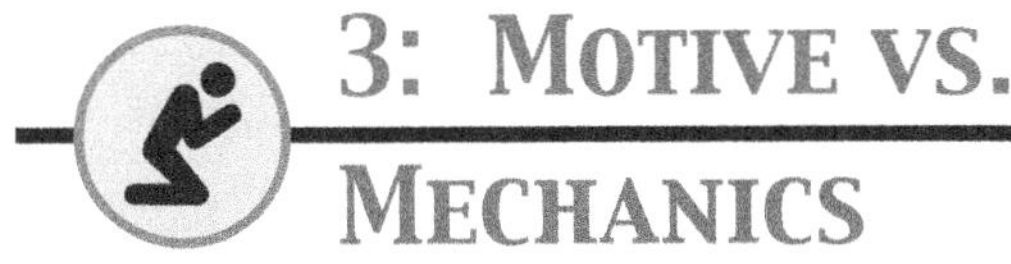

3: Motive vs. Mechanics

How and Why

In every endeavor (including prayer) *why* matters more than *how,* for without purpose, process would never develop. Invention afterall, is not the mother of necessity. Thus process must always serve purpose. In prayer then before we can address the mechanics of "how to" we must give our attention to answering "what for." What is our purpose in prayer? The answer of why will determine all our subsequent how's.

It was popular some years ago to pray the prayer offered by an Old Testament man named Jabez as if it were some magical incantation to get more stuff and to avoid pain—what rubbish! Jabez's prayer was fine for him; the Lord answered it. But why pray Jabez's prayer unless you want what Jabez wanted? Do you desire to be like Jabez?

Let your motivation for prayer be the same desire that compelled Moses to the top of Sinai and was revealed when he asked, **"If I have found favor in Thy sight, let me know Thy ways, that I may know Thee, so that I may find favor in Thy sight"** (Exodus 33:13). Moses' request to see God's face was an expression of his desire—his why—to know God. Though prayer is the conduit for our appeals, thanksgivings, and praises, that conversation is chiefly our means of relationship with God, for, **"Thus the LORD used to speak to Moses face to face, just as a man speaks to his friend"** (Exodus 33:11).

Personalized Prayer

When our purpose becomes intense enough, the process will follow, because people always find a way to get what they really want. Before Jen and I were married, I wanted to know everything about her and to "find favor in her sight." To that end, we made opportunities to spend time together. Conversation came easily and our relationship grew. After nearly thirty years, I'm still learning about her, and regular conversation remains the daily bread of our marriage. In the same way, if we want to know God, we will make time to pray. The mechanics will follow.

If someone observed my marriage and wanted one just like it, they would be disappointed. It's impossible for anyone to have my marriage, because they're not married to my wife or to her husband. Our relationship works for us because it's ours. If someone tried to emulate what we do in every meticulous detail, the results might well be disastrous for them. Neither relationships nor prayers are one-size-fits-all copy-and-paste propositions.

Prayer too is a learn-by-doing exercise. Like fly casting, there comes a point when instruction can take you no farther. Only when you have the rod in your own hand and feel the outstretched line load it for the forward cast do you begin to truly learn. Similarly, I can give you principles, but I cannot teach you what to pray; prayer is relationship more than recipe.

Having said that, certain principles are common to all relationships and, along with some simple tips, help us deepen our relationship with God. The following may well be the most important.

Three Little Words

Looking back over the long years of their marriage, an old man once said to his wife, "If I had a dollar for every time I said, 'I love you'… I would have said it a lot more often." ;) HaHa! I love that joke, but there's a kernel of truth beneath the punch line. It's easy to neglect those words.

After almost thirty years of wedded bliss, my wife still appreciates it when I say "I love you." It brightens her soul to be reassured that my feelings and commitment to her remain unchanged. Even though she benefits from receiving the tender affirmation, in this case also it is true that the giver is more blessed than the receiver, since the speaker is changed more by those words than the hearer.

James 3:3–5 describes the tongue as the rudder of your life, because what you speak directs what you do and how you feel. This is true in every aspect of prayer, but I notice that folks often find it uncomfortable or even difficult to tell God that they love Him. Praise, petition, and penitence come easier to the timid heart than speaking those three little words. Remember the first time you confessed to your beloved, "I love you?"

In prayer, as in marriage, it can be easy to slip into the routine of daily tasks and neglect the confession of love that should be the reason for our conversation with God in the first place. Though it may sound strange, make it a habit to tell the Lord—and your spouse—that you love them. You'll be surprised by how it changes you.

Reflection Questions

- Before we can answer the how of prayer we must understand the ____________.
- Compare the motives of Jabez and Moses in prayer. Of the two, which do you think would have had the more fulfilling relationship with God and why? ____________

  ____

  ____
- Why would it be impossible for someone else to have your relationship with God? ____________________

  ____

  ____
- If the tongue is a rudder of the soul, what ought to be spoken to God? ____________________
- Do you feel awkward telling God that you love Him? Why or why not? ____________________

  ____

4: Does God Hear?

A Word of Encouragement

If your prayers are awkward and make you self-conscious, you're doing it right. These feelings are not the goal of our time spent with God, but they do indicate that we're praying with purpose—seeking significant interaction with the Lord. Conversation is often difficult when beginning a relationship and more so when restoring one; if you're uncomfortable, your prayers are likely forcing you to face the Lord and yourself honestly. The previous devotion discussed pursuing that relationship by committing the time. If you're making the effort, well done. Keep it up! If not, pause now and take the next few minutes to pray before continuing this lesson. Just give it your best shot. Five or ten minutes with the Lord is a far better use of your time than completing the next few pages.

Hello?

Does God hear me when I pray? It's hard to be consistent in prayer without the assurance that those prayers are being heard on the receiving end. David often requests the Lord's attention and praises Him for it. **"Give ear to my prayer,"** he writes in Psalm 17:1. **"I have called upon Thee, for Thou wilt answer me, O God"** (v. 6). Jesus says your Father recognizes your prayers even in secret (Matthew 6:6), and John is more emphatic, **"And this is the confidence which we have before Him, that, if we ask anything according to His will, He hears us"** (1 John 5:14).

Consider for a moment what we so easily take for granted. Isaiah shuddered to find himself in the presence of the Almighty. "Woe is me!" said the imperfect prophet (Isaiah 6:5). Yet a child of God has confidence in the Lord's presence to ask anything according to His will and be heard. **"Let us therefore draw near with confidence to**

the throne of grace, that we may receive mercy and may find grace to help in time of need" (Hebrews 4:16). God grants that access and invites His child to cast **"all your anxiety upon Him, because He cares for you"** (1 Peter 5:7). God *wants* to hear.

Prayers of Sinners

Sin is a formidable obstacle to prayer. **"Your sins have hidden His face from you, so that He does not hear"** (Isaiah 59:2). Does God hear the prayers of sinners? Certainly He does, but not in the same way that He hears those who are forgiven in Christ. The latter enjoy the intercession of the Holy Spirit (which we shall discuss later) and the confidence to receive grace as previously mentioned in Hebrews 4:16.

God hears the prayers of Saul of Tarsus in Acts 9 and Cornelius in Acts 10. Both those men are outside of Christ when they pray; they had not yet become Christians, however, their prayers do not go unnoticed by the Lord. Furthermore, God responds to those prayers; He sends someone to those praying men to preach the gospel.

Here's another twist. What about the Old Testament faithful? Their sins remained unaddressed under the Old Covenant prior to Christ, for He is their sacrifice as well (Hebrews 9:15). Yet the Lord answers them. Categorical forgiveness, then, is not the only factor we must consider when determining whether our prayers are heard—relationship is key.

Israel was God's chosen people, but because they had neglected Him, their prayers often fell on deaf ears (Proverbs 1:24–28). Likewise, baptism does not guarantee an audience with God any more than a wedding ring ensures a listening ear from your spouse. The Lord looks for honesty, humility, and authenticity. **"Then you will call, and the LORD will answer"** (Isaiah 58:1–9).

Reflection Questions

- If you told God that you feel awkward when praying, and He answered you audibly, what do you think He might say?

  ____

  ____

- On a scale of 0% to 100%, how confident are you that God hears and is attentive to your prayers? __________

- Which passage of the Scriptures gives you the most assurance that God takes an active interest in your prayers? You may choose from the lesson or write one of your own complete with chapter and verse below.

  ____

- Based on the examples of Saul and Cornelius, how is God likely to answer the prayers of someone outside of Christ?

  ____

- Honesty, humility, and authenticity—which one comes most easily for you in prayer, and which requires the most effort?

  ____

  ____

5: The Spirit Intercedes

Inspired Prayers

Believe it or not, I am often at a loss for words. When it comes to prayer, **"we do not know how to pray as we should,"** and for this reason, the Lord steps in to help our weakness. **"The Spirit Himself intercedes for us with groanings too deep for words"** (Romans 8:26). This human weakness—our incomplete understanding of the situation and our ignorance of what the Lord is trying to accomplish—limits our prayers in two ways: what to pray for, and how to pray for it. Many times we do not know God's will in a specific circumstance. Thus, it's easy to default in our prayers to the habits we've formed: "Thank you for this, guide us in that, et cetera, et cetera, blah, blah, blah." The result can become mechanical and repetitive.

The Scriptures are a great help to us as the basis from which to pray. We will discuss this topic more thoroughly in the coming lessons, but it deserves a mention here. The Bible, both Old and New Testament, is filled with examples of how to pray. The Psalms, for instance, are the prayers of men inspired by the same Spirit who aids us in ours. To use these as the context from which to pray prevents robotic prayers and ensures that we are in fact praying according to His will.

God Hears

Jesus warns His disciples against babbling prayers, **"Therefore do not be like them; for your Father knows what you need, before you ask Him"** (Matthew 6:8). Even before my prayers are formed, the Lord knows what I need. In the case of small children who are unable to verbalize their needs and desires, their vocalization is generally the same for every want—

legitimate or otherwise—they cry. In the case of my own children, these cries all sounded much the same to me. However, my wife Jen could tell the difference. She could distinguish the sound of a hungry cry from a diaper cry or a sleepy cry. Thankfully, God knows our needs apart from our ability to recognize or even ask for them.

We see a glimpse of this in the way Jesus worked with the people of His day. He often addressed their need rather than their request. When Nicodemus came to Him, the ruler of Israel said, **"We know that You have come from God as a teacher..."** (John 3:2) But Jesus' answer addressed his unspoken need, **"... truly, truly, I say to you, unless one is born again he cannot see the kingdom of God."** (John 3:3) It's doubtful that the Pharisee came looking for that information, but it was what he needed.

Our Mediator

Christ is our intercessor. In the pattern of the Old Testament high priest, He is the mediator between God and man, and in that role He is the liaison through whom we speak to God. **"Christ Jesus is He who died, yes, rather who was raised, who is at the right hand of God, who also intercedes for us"** (Romans 8:34). Our needs and requests come into the Lord's ears, as it were, through the council of Christ, who has demonstrated His empathy toward humanity through the incarnation. He knows what it's like to live in the flesh so that as a merciful and faithful high priest, **"He is able to save forever those who draw near to God through Him, since He always lives to make intercession for them"** (Hebrews 7:25). Be confident that whatever you ask, God hears and answers according to your need.

Reflection Questions

- If you could see each situation from God's perspective, how might it change your prayers?____________________

  ____

- In what Bible book specifically might one find examples of inspired prayers to aid in formulating one's own according to God's will? __________________________________

- Is God limited by my ability to understand or verbalize my genuine needs? __________

- If God were to address my primary need, what issue might He deal with first?

  ____

- Jesus intercedes for us before God. What experience makes Him the perfect "man" for the job?

  ____

6: Do I Have Enough Faith?

Incredible Promise

Though they would not admit it, most Christians do not believe Jesus' promise: **"Truly I say to you, if you have faith, and do not doubt, you shall not only do what was done to the fig tree, but even if you say to this mountain, 'Be taken up and cast into the sea,' it shall happen. And all things you ask in prayer, believing, you shall receive"** (Matthew 21:21-22). It simply sounds too good to be true, so Christians find reasons to excuse unmoving mountains and to content themselves instead with molehills.

[Sarcasm] New Christians present a special challenge. They have a naive tendency to believe that God can and will grant the requests they have asked of Him. They need the benefit of the more mature and jaded in the faith to prevent disappointment. ;)

Sound foolish? Jaded faith is no faith at all. What mountains have you requested God to move lately? Jesus is just as serious about this promise as any other.

Unbelief

For the skeptic and the doubter, there is an escape clause—"if you have faith." This devilish loophole allows faith healers and other charlatans to lay the blame for their failures on the very ones they claim to help. Jesus' promise is limited, they say, to those with enough faith. Therefore, to move mountainous things, mountainous faith is required. Au contraire. **"For truly I say to you, if you have faith as a mustard seed, you shall say to this mountain, 'Move from here to there,' and it shall move; and**

nothing shall be impossible to you" (Matthew 17:20). Let's consider some examples of small faith.

Jairus is a synagogue official whose daughter is near death. In desperation he seeks out Jesus, but before they can return to the house, the little girl has passed. The onlookers' faith fails: **"Your daughter has died; do not trouble the Teacher anymore"** (Luke 8:49). On another occasion a boy is possessed. The child's father almost hopelessly turns to Jesus, **"But if you can do anything, take pity on us and help us!"** (Mark 9:22). Even Jesus is taken aback by this meager vote of confidence. The Savior asks incredulously, **"If you can?"**

But perhaps the best example (and the most humorous) is provided by the early Church. King Herod arrests Peter with the intention of executing him the following day. For that reason, **"prayer for him was being made fervently by the church to God"** (Acts 12:5). Unbeknownst to the praying church, an angel frees Peter from prison and leads the muddled apostle to the very house where they are gathered in prayer on his behalf. However, upon Peter's arrival, they are unwilling to accept that their prayers have been answered or that Peter is knocking on the door. They would sooner believe their servant girl crazy or Peter already dead than that God has moved their mountain (Acts 12:15–16).

Enough Faith

We would not consider any of the above as examples of great faith, *yet they all received what they asked for*. Why?

Some years ago, I made an investigation of Jesus' interactions with those who sought to receive something from Him. By correlating those results, I had hoped to find the "secret ingredient" to answered prayer and the answer to our topic today —how much faith is enough to receive?

In every case where the Savior is asked to heal a child, cast out a demon, restore sight, et cetera, I found a surprising trend. The answer is always yes. Everyone who requests of Jesus (either in person or in prayer) receives what they ask for. The only exceptions are requests for free lunches, family interventions, and parlor tricks. Even the persistent Canaanite woman eventually gets what she came for (Matthew 15:28). What measure of faith did they all have in common? Enough to ask. **"Ask, and it shall be given to you; seek, and you shall find; knock, and it shall be opened to you"** (Matthew 7:7). Simply put, the faith to ask is sufficient faith to receive.

We may pray, then, with mountainous confidence fully assured that we have the requests we have asked of Him. And if so—that is to say, if we now truly expect great things—how might we pray?

When Jesus comes to His hometown of Nazareth, He is met with unbelief (Mark 6:1–6). His neighbors know Him as Mary's son, the carpenter. **"And He could do no miracle there except that He laid His hands upon a few sick people and healed them"** (v. 5). Why can nothing more be done? I am forced to conclude that it is because they do not ask. Their familiarity with Jesus blinds them to what He is ready to do.

I can't help but notice an uncomfortable resemblance. Those for whom Jesus has become commonplace do not seek to move mountains. Like the residents of Nazareth, they are content with the healing of a few sick people, but dare to ask nothing more. They do not have because they do not ask (James 4:2). You have sufficient faith. Dare to pray.

Reflection Questions

- Summarize Jesus' too-good-to-be-true promise.

  ____

- What flimsy excuse might be shared by faith healers and Christians alike to explain a lack of results in their life?

  ____

- What sort of faith is required to move mountainous things? ______________________________________

- How many of the people who came to Jesus with a legitimate need were refused? ____________________

- How much faith is sufficient to receive? ____________

- How will your prayers change with the confidence that you have enough faith? __________________________

- Jesus is unconcerned with geological topography. What mountains would He like to move in your life?

  ____

  ____

7: Asking in Faith

Philosophy of Prayer

"Ask, and it shall be given to you; seek, and you shall find; knock, and it shall be opened to you" (Matthew 7:7). Everyone would like to ensure their prayers are heard and answered, and we will consider this topic for the next several lessons. However, before we can resolve that question fully, we must take a little time today and address some fundamental principles of prayer. Let's discuss how God answers, and, yes, even His limitations.

Indulge me a slight but necessary tangent. One of the most prominent obstacles to Christianity in American culture is what I will call "subjective faith." It is the child of postmodern philosophy and religious tradition, having inherited from the latter the appearance of Christianity and from the former the beliefs that absolutes do not exist; that the world is not rational; and that it does not operate by unchanging, understandable laws. I can hear some of you rolling your eyes. ;) Bear with me a little more. This has everything to do with your prayers.

This subjective faith in modern western religion has embraced the ideas that all spiritual principles are open to personal interpretation and that truth is in the mind of the beholder. Adherents have welcomed the notion that faith picks up where reason leaves off, rendering their faith blind and the world rightly wary of such superstitious humbug.

Joe Christian

If observation and reason are ignored, then experience is the only remaining guide. Nowhere is this more evident than in the religious world, which seeks God based on its emotional perception of closeness to Him, interpreted through circumstances. I will explain.

On Monday morning, Joe Christian knows he is close to God because yesterday's service was particularly moving. Joe was touched by what he experienced at his worship center and believes he made a connection with God. Joe prays, "Lord, guide me and bless me today. Help me to do Your will." Then he looks for God's answer.

On the way to work, the ratio of green lights to red is higher than usual. Someone left doughnuts in the break room, and he leaves work a little early. Joe considers his blessings and concludes he must be in God's will.

Joe is full of hogwash. All of his conclusions about the past two days are entirely subjective. If tomorrow Joe prays the same and is delayed in traffic, develops the stomach flu, and has to work late, is he outside of God's will? Have his prayers been rejected?

If New Testament Christians, Paul the apostle, or Jesus Himself looked to their circumstances as proof that the Lord was pleased with them, what would they have concluded? Or conversely, if modern Christians found themselves in the circumstances endured by their first-century brethren, they might falsely conclude their prayers had gone unanswered—or worse—that the Lord was punishing them for some lack of faith. This is self-serving madness.

Confident Requests

How do I know my prayers are answered? Experience alone cannot provide objective confirmation that our requests have been granted, since, like Joe's, they are subject to personal interpretation. God is free to answer yes, no, perhaps, or not now, and it is utterly impossible for someone to determine by circumstance alone which of those answers he or she has received. Then, you may rightly ask, what confidence do we have? If you're ready to throw up your praying hands in frustration, read on.

The objective foundation for Christianity is the authority of God's Word—not our experience. Its validity can be tested, its accuracy measured, and its claims confirmed. Reasoned faith must begin there. If the Scriptures can be trusted, then we can rationally enjoy the confidence John describes: **"This is the confidence which we have before Him, that, if we ask anything according to His will, He hears us. And if we know that He hears us in whatever we ask, we know that we have the requests which we have asked from Him"** (1 John 5:14–15).

Joe Christian's problem is not his prayers or his faith, but where his faith is placed. He interprets the Scriptures' promises through the lens of his circumstances, attempting to read the tea leaves in traffic lights. Joe needs to reverse that relationship and interpret his circumstances through the objective lens of the Scriptures.

If God says He hears us, then we can be sure our prayers have reached the Almighty and that He has answered in the way that is best for us according to His will. We will discuss what it means to ask according to His will in a later lesson, but we can be totally confident—whatever our circumstances—that God not only hears, but grants our request that His will be done.

It is precisely at those times, when our plight is the most trying, when our situation seems direst, when hope appears lost, that our confidence in God's attentive grace is needed most. Consider this example: Jesus fervently prays three times in Gethsemane, **"saying, 'Father, if Thou art willing, remove this cup from Me; yet not My will, but Thine be done'"** (Luke 22:42). The Father's voice does not thunder in reply from heaven nor do angels appear to lead the way. Is Jesus' prayer heard? Of course it is. But how could the Savior know God's answer? Is there another way? Might this cup pass from Him? God's answer becomes clear when the soldiers break the solitude of the garden and ask for Jesus of Nazareth. Jesus learned God's will just as we do—*our circumstances are God's answer.*

One final note: God is limited in the way He can work with us by how we respond to His efforts. If God did confirm our requests by miraculous signs, two problems would result. First, many would follow Christ for the gifts and not for their giver. Second, if praying produced a voice from heaven or a wet or dry fleece as in the case of Gideon, it would be a step backward from God's ultimate goal of producing faith in Him, rather than in the sign.

Be assured that God hears and grants your requests, and that your circumstances are His answer.

Reflection Questions

- Describe the term "subjective faith" as used in this lesson.

  ____

- If I judged my relationship with God on the basis of my circumstances, what would I conclude?

  ____

- Is that a rational conclusion? ______________________

- Upon what firm foundation does our confidence in prayer rest? ______________________________________

  ____

- Describe the proper relationship between faith and circumstance in determining whether God hears and answers our prayers. ______________________________

  ____

- If Jesus had looked only at His circumstances to determine if His prayers were heard, what might He have concluded? ____________________________________

- Objectively speaking, in what way does God reveal His will and the answer of our prayers to us? ________________

  ____

8: Watch and Pray

Staying Alert in Prayer

Have you ever fallen asleep while you're praying? The Scriptures exhort us to stay alert in prayer, but it has nothing to do with caffeine. Let's learn exactly what it does mean and how we can complete the armor of God **"with all perseverance and petition for all the saints"** (Ephesians 6:18).

When Jesus knows the time of His betrayal is growing near, He moves off into the garden of Gethsemane where He will be undisturbed for a time, and He appoints three watchmen. Leaving all but the trio of Peter, James, and John, He goes a little further and speaks to the three, **"My soul is deeply grieved, to the point of death; remain here and keep watch with Me"** (Matthew 26:38). Jesus Himself goes a stone's throw from them and begins to pray. After an hour in prayer, He returns to the snoozing disciples. **"So, you men could not keep watch with Me for one hour? Keep watching and praying, that you may not enter into temptation; the spirit is willing, but the flesh is weak"** (v. 40–41).

Keeping Watch

Peter, James, and John are instructed to keep watch, but what are they watching for? The imminent threat of arrest is certainly on Jesus' mind. Perhaps He cleverly positions the eight disciples as an outer perimeter and the three as a final warning of Judas' arrival flanked by soldiers from the chief priest. However, this explanation is unsatisfactory, because escape is never Jesus' intent, and He is hardly surprised by the soldiers He knows are coming.

Consider these two clues provided by Jesus. First, they are to keep watch *with Jesus*; that is to say, Jesus is also keeping watch. Second, their vigil serves to keep them from temptation. Jesus isn't watching for the soldiers; He is fervently in prayer staving off temptation—His sweat like drops of blood. Prayer therefore is the means by which the soldier of God remains spiritually alert.

Prayer and Petition

Now that we know what we're looking for, let's consider that verse again.

Ephesians 6:18

"With all PRAYER and *petition* pray **at all times** in the Spirit...	BE ON THE ALERT with all **perseverance** and *petition* for all the saints."

Notice that the verse is a mirror image of itself, repeating the same three elements in the first and second halves. For clarity I have identified the corresponding components with matching typefaces. When we compare the two halves, we find that the piece that corresponds to prayer is "be on the alert!"

Similar instructions are written to the Colossians, confirming our conclusion: **"Devote yourselves to prayer, keeping alert in it with an attitude of thanksgiving"** (Colossians 4:2).

A soldier armed to the teeth as described in Ephesians 6 is of little value while he sleeps. Likewise, a Christian may possess the whole armor of God, but without prayer his spiritual eyes remain closed. When Jesus returns, may He find us all watching and praying.

Reflection Questions

- According to Matthew 26:40–41, what did Jesus encourage the disciples to watch for?

  ____

- Jesus was also keeping watch. How was He doing so?

  ____

- Match each element of the first half of Eph 6:18 to its corresponding part from the second half.

at all times	petition
petition	on the alert
prayer	perseverance

- Watchful prayer concerns content and consistency. Which of those two elements would help you most to be more spiritually alert? ______________________________

- Describe a sleeping soldier.

  ____

  ____

9: Spotting Temptation through Prayer

A Note on Sin

Jesus exhorted His disciples to watch and pray. In our previous devotion, we learned how prayer is the means by which the Christian keeps his spiritual eyes open. Like well-armed soldiers, we are encouraged to keep alert in prayer with an attitude of thanksgiving (Colossians 4:2). Let's consider how prayer keeps us alert that we may not enter into temptation.

First, a note about sin. All sin at its most basic level usurps the place that belongs to God. From the first, the tempter subtly invites Eve to occupy a place that does not belong to her. **"You surely shall not die!"** he lies. **"For God knows that in the day you eat from it your eyes will be opened, and you will be like God, knowing good and evil"** (Genesis 3:4–5). Eve takes the bait and wistfully notes, **"that the tree was desirable to make one wise"** (Genesis 3:6).

Eve is tempted by the intrinsic pleasure of the fruit, its visual appeal—and the promise that she would be like God. Those are respectively what John describes as: the lust of the flesh, the lust of the eyes, and the boastful pride of life (1 John 2:16), and prayer is the key to withstanding their siren call.

Humble Resistance

When Jesus dealt with temptation, He did so just as you and I must. That is to say, He was **"tempted in all things as we are, yet without sin"** (Hebrews 4:15). Jesus didn't have it easy; He had to resist the same appeals to the lusts of the flesh and eyes and to boastful pride just as we do. How did He manage it?

The record of Jesus' duel with the devil found in Matthew 4:1–11 and Luke 4:1–13 gives us important insight. Notice that the tempter includes all three categories of sin. First he proffers to the flesh: "command that these stones become bread." Next, he appeals to the pride of life: "If You are the Son of God, throw Yourself down." Finally, he brings all the glory of earth before the Lord's eyes: "All these things will I give You." How could the Son of God resist, and how shall we do likewise?

The power to resist temptation is humility, for God gives help to the humble: **"Submit therefore to God. Resist the devil and he will flee from you"** (James 4:7). Likewise 1 Peter 5:6–9 combines humility, alertness, and resistance for a potent defense against sin. **"Humble yourselves, therefore, under the mighty hand of God... Be of sober *spirit,* be on the alert. Your adversary, the devil, prowls about like a roaring lion, seeking someone to devour. But resist him, firm in *your* faith."** The same recipe for resistance can be found in 1 Corinthians 10:12–13 along with a poignant warning.

Practiced Prayer

Jesus resists temptation the same way. His humility is well-practiced. In fact, we find His secret in the Lord's prayer of Matthew 6. Jesus knows it is not for Him to transform the stones into loaves, for He recognizes His Father as provider when He prays, **"Give us this day our daily bread"** (Matthew 6:11). Jesus does not succumb to a temple leap, for He prays, **"Thy kingdom come. Thy will be done, on earth as it is in heaven"** (Matthew 6:10). And since He prays, **"Our Father who art in heaven, hallowed be Thy name"** (Matthew 6:9), it would be wrong to worship the name or authority of another.

The scriptures Jesus uses to resist the devil's wiles all humbly confirm the place of God just as His prayers do also. When we pray, we come face to face with the person of God, and we reaffirm His place as our provider, protector, and Lord. If our eyes are open to His position, the subtle enticements to put ourselves in His place (read sin) are more readily apparent.

The entanglements of sin can be identified and overcome with the humility practiced through prayer.

Reflection Questions

- What subtle invitation is at the core of all temptation?

  ____

- The lust of the flesh (comfort/pleasure), the lust of the eyes (greed/envy), and the pride of life (power/control) appeal to human arrogance. Which is the most troublesome for you and why? ______________

  ____

- What virtue provides the power to resist temptation?

  ____

- How did Jesus regularly practice resistance to temptation?

  ____

  ____

- How can you reaffirm God's rightful place as your provider, protecter, and Lord?

  ____

- What is the most helpful truth you learned today?

  ____

  ____

10: Magic Words of Prayer

Abracadabra

The Lord wants us to have confidence when we pray—confidence that He hears and confidence that He answers. Three elements are necessary for our prayers to be heard and answered: faith, agreement, and motive. We discussed the role of faith in our prayers in lessons 5 and 6, and James sums it up nicely, **"You do not have because you do not ask"** (James 4:2). For the next few lessons, let's discuss what it means to agree with God in our prayers. Before we can delve too deeply, we must first dispel a myth.

Jesus said it twice for emphasis: **"And whatever you ask in My name, that will I do, that the Father may be glorified in the Son. If you ask Me anything in My name, I will do it"** (John 14:13-14). This is why every prayer ends in the magic words, "In Jesus' name, amen." Christians know that without that tiny incantation added to their wish list, their requests don't stand a chance. ;)

Dispelling Mantras

Though miraculous, prayer is not magical. Magic implies tapping into a power not your own—hacking a system to exploit it for some unsanctioned benefit. The sons of Sceva attempt this in Acts 19:13 when they mistakenly think that invoking the names of Jesus and Paul will make the demon obey.

Prayer is nothing like that, yet it's not uncommon for Christians to approach prayer as if it is a spell to be cast for good luck and warding off temptation. They attempt to find the right words uttered in the right order—perhaps the prayer of Jabez or the Lord's Prayer—to make the magic work. They have become preoccupied with the getting and fail to appreciate the Giver.

Perhaps we have misunderstood Jesus' instruction to pray in His name, for upon closer inspection we find that Jesus Himself never uses those words in His prayers. Maybe it would have been redundant for Jesus to pray in His own name, but neither the apostles nor their disciples do either. Either Jesus does not take His own advice and it is ignored by the early Church, or He means something else by it entirely.

Name of Jesus

"Open up in the name of the king!" Such a command was appropriate from the sheriff of Nottingham when the highest authority in the land was the king. A significant change was found in America before the time of kings returned, where the command became, "Open up in the name of the law." Since the Constitution rather than a king was the chief authority in that new land, those acting on its behalf appeal to rule—not ruler—as the rightful source of their jurisdiction. This usage of "in the name" has sadly fallen out of fashion in modern English creating some confusion.

The high priest questions Peter and John before the Sanhedrin. The council inquires, **"By what power, or in what name, have you done this?"** (Acts 4:7). The chief apostle answers, **"Let it be known to all of you... that by the name of Jesus Christ the Nazarene, whom you crucified, whom God raised from the dead—by this name this man stands here before you in good health"** (Acts 4:10). The miracle has come through the name of Jesus, but does Peter suppose that the mere utterance of "Jesus" has caused the man to stand? Not at all. Rather the council asks and Peter answers the question of authority. By whose authority have they acted? They would answer that question again in Acts 5:28–30.

Likewise, Jesus speaks to the issue of authority in the Great Commission, **"All authority has been given to Me in heaven and on earth. Go therefore and make disciples of all the nations, baptizing them in the name of the Father and the Son and the**

Holy Spirit" (Matthew 28:18–19). Thus, the commission is carried out "in the name of Jesus"—by His authority. **"And Peter said to them, 'Repent, and let each of you be baptized in the name of Jesus Christ for the forgiveness of your sins; and you shall receive the gift of the Holy Spirit'"** (Acts 2:38).

To pray in Jesus' name means to entreat the Lord by the authority of Christ. To add the traditional tagline, "in Jesus' name, amen," to our daily prayers does not violate the principle, but it is not strictly necessary. It should, however, remind us by whose authority we have a right to speak to the Almighty, not serve as a charm for receiving our requests.

Reflection Questions

- What are the three components of effective prayer?

  ____

  ____

  ____

- Why do you think Christians sometimes approach prayer as if it were a magical spell to be cast rather than a relationship with God? ____________________________

  ____

- What words do we find conspicuously absent from Jesus' recorded prayers and those of His disciples?

  ____

- What does the term *in the name* mean?

  ____

- Jesus instructs us, "If you ask Me anything in My name, I will do it." How does Jesus want us to pray?

  ____

- If you were specially authorized by Jesus Christ to speak to God, would you be confident to do so? ______

- Have you been so authorized? _______

11: His Name, His Will

Calling on His Name

When the Scriptures use the term *the name of Jesus,* it means more than simple pronunciation. Consider Philippians 2:10: **"That at the name of Jesus every knee should bow, of those who are in heaven, and on earth, and under the earth."** How foolish to think that the manipulation of tongue and lips by mortal men could cause such obeisance throughout all creation. It is the presence and authority of the One who sits on the throne from whom heaven and earth flee (Revelation 20:11) rather than the verbalization of His name to which every knee must bow.

Name refers to the honor and authority of its bearer. We have a term in English that better resembles that traditional usage. Modern speakers are accustomed to the term *title,* which carries the meaning of both name and authority. Goliath learned humility too late when a ruddy youth came to him, **"in the name of the Lord of hosts... whom you have taunted"** (1 Samuel 17:45). It wasn't the pronunciation of *Yahweh* that Goliath had defied, but His authority.

That usage of *in the name* continues into the New Testament, for conversion occurs "in the name of Jesus Christ" (Acts 2:38). It is upon this name that we call/appeal (see also Acts 22:16, Romans 10:13, Acts 9:14). "But what," you may ask, "does any of this have to do with my prayers being answered?" Everything.

Name and Will

Jesus promised in John 14:13–14, **"And whatever you ask in My name, that will I do, that the Father may be glorified in the Son. If you ask Me anything in My name, I will do it."** In our last lesson, we discussed what this does not mean. Today let's consider what it does.

The same assurance of answered prayer is given to us again: **"This is the confidence which we have before Him, that, if we ask anything according to His will, He hears us. And if we know that He hears us in whatever we ask, we know that we have the requests which we have asked from Him"** (1 John 5:14–15). Notice the strong resemblance to the John 14 passage. In the former, *in My name* is the key ingredient for answered prayer; the latter identifies it as asking according to His will. The two are equivalent terms; *in His name* means *according to His will.*

Business of Prayer

Consider a construction foreman or a traveling salesman. There are certain expenses each incur as a consequence of fulfilling their responsibilities. For these expenditures the two have authority to act as agents of the company. Both men are free to act in the interest of the business they represent and in the company's name to make requests. However, far from enjoying carte blanche, they must make requisitions within the parameters of their job descriptions. The salesman may not purchase a boat for "entertaining clients" any more than the foreman may swipe the company card for a new hunting rifle. They are constrained in their requests by the will of the company they represent.

The ambassador of Christ is likewise free to request whatever is necessary and prudent to accomplish the task before him in full confidence that such requests will be honored—even if a mountain must move. In the business of prayer, the will and the authority (name) of the boss are one and the same. But to answer the question, "What may I pray for?", we must ask another: "What business should I be about?"

It is in such confidence that David approaches Goliath. Unbeknownst to all but Samuel and David's immediate family, the Bethlehem shepherd has quietly been anointed king. When the super-sized Philistine challenges the armies of Israel and taunts their God, who should champion their cause but the king? David has been given authority by God, and he exercises that title when acting according to the Lord's will. God moves a mountain of a man, and the giant falls.

Reflection Questions

- What modern English word more accurately reflects the meaning of the biblical term *name?* ________________

- What two parallel passages suggest that *in His name* means *according to His will?* ________________________________

  ____

- What sort of requests might a salesman—and a child of God—get approved ____________________________

- Why was David successful against Goliath? __________

  ____

- What authority has God given you to exercise on His behalf?

  ____

12: Requests God Grants

Desires of your Heart

"Delight yourself in the LORD; And He will give you the desires of your heart" (Psalm 37:4). It's easy to focus on our desires and view prayer as a means to that end. Three elements are necessary to ensure our prayers are heard and answered. We have discussed sufficient faith and agreement with God, so today let's consider the third element of successful prayer: motive.

Motive rightly brings us back to relationship. Our Lord is not a vending machine issuing favors when the correct buttons are pressed. Neither must we, like Jacob, wrestle blessings from Him as though He were our adversary. God wants to give good gifts to His children (Matthew 7:7–11), and He wants His children to desire them.

Not My Will

Jesus' instruction on the mountain and His prayer in the garden have a common theme. He teaches His disciples to pray, **"Thy kingdom come. Thy will be done, on earth as it is in heaven"** (Matthew 6:10). Later, the Lord makes a similar request, **"saying, 'Father, if Thou art willing, remove this cup from Me; yet not My will, but Thine be done'"** (Luke 22:42). When we pray our goal must not be merely to get what we want, but to want what we get.

We know (objectively) that God's will really is best for us, for others, and for the Church. Isn't that what we genuinely desire? Jesus' flesh did not relish the prospect of the cross, but He wanted the Father's will more than He wished to avoid the trial before Him. When we pray, we must pray this way. God does not grant requests that are contrary to His will and therefore to our detriment. **"You ask and do not receive, because you ask with**

wrong motives, so that you may spend it on your pleasures" (James 4:3). Thus, our prayers must echo those of Jesus, "Not my will but Yours be done."

What I Know and What I Don't

You may not want me to pray for your sickly aunt Edna. Though your request might be for healing, I will pray that God's will be done, and I should warn you—I haven't the foggiest idea what that means for Edna. Perhaps it would be best for her to recover, but it might also be that her condition is developing character in Edna, and she should remain ill. On the other hand, it might best serve the kingdom for others to learn to care for her, or that through her condition doors for the gospel could be opened, and she should get worse. Or perhaps it would be best for the old bird to finally die. I simply cannot know. However, we can pray that Edna (and many others) would be healed if possible, but even more that God's will would be done.

Some cases are clearer. **"For the Son of Man has come to seek and to save that which was lost"** (Luke 19:10). I know that as Christians we carry on the work of Christ; seeking and saving are what we ought to be about. I can therefore pray with confidence that the Lord would make His people in general, and myself in particular, more effective in that endeavor. I can pray that God would open doors for the word, that I may speak it clearly and with boldness, that I would be wise and make the most of the opportunities with those outside of Christ, responding with grace (Colossians 4:3–5). Such a prayer will be answered, for I know it is the will of God. If I truly "delight myself in the Lord," the desires of my heart will be His desires (Psalm 37:4).

Reflection Questions

- What are the three ingredients of effective prayer? (For help, see lesson 9.) ______________________________

____

- On what should we base our requests to God?

____

- Why do we want His blessing, and why does He desire to give it? ______________________________

____

- What is best for Aunt Edna? ______________________

____

- Why did Jesus desire God's will more than His own?

____

____

- From Colossians 4:3–5 identify one component of God's will for you. ______________________________

- Write the personal application of the request you might ask with confidence based on God's will.

____

13: Why Ask?

I Knew That

God always has a reason for doing what appears to us perplexing. Consider the redundancy of prayer. **"Do not be anxious then, saying, 'What shall we eat?' or 'What shall we drink?' or 'With what shall we clothe ourselves?' For all these things the Gentiles eagerly seek; for your heavenly Father knows that you need all these things"** (Matthew 6:31–32). Think how much time would be saved if God—who knows what we need anyway—just provided in advance what He instructs us to ask, seek, and knock for. Besides, He knows our needs better than we do. Yet still, the Omniscient invites us to ask. Perhaps He knows something we don't.

Certainly, God does not need reminders as though He might forget that we are hungry, thirsty, or poorly clothed. It is safe also to conclude that the Lord is not indulging ego as His people grovel for their basic necessities. If such prayers are not for His benefit, it follows that we have something to gain from the exercise.

Brats

I cannot abide spoiled children. They view themselves as superior to every authority and deserving of their every desire. Though slaves, their snotty airs and greedy fingers have known neither want nor gratitude. This unsavory description fits Israel nicely upon their exit from Egypt. After three days in the wilderness without water, **"the people grumbled at Moses, saying, 'What shall we drink?'"** (Exodus 15:24). Did God know they were thirsty? Of course. Why then, didn't He provide for them to drink? God was waiting to be asked.

The Hebrews are slow learners. They repeat their grumbling when hungry (Exodus 16:2–3) and again when thirst returns. They demand that Moses provide for them and grumble in their need. **"Why do you quarrel with me?"** Moses asks. **"Why do you test the LORD?"** (Exodus 17:2). As before, the Lord waits (knowing their need) until they ask.

As a wise father, the Lord knows how His children benefit from acknowledging their need and indebtedness. *Please* and *thank you* instill children with respectful confidence and humility. Asking in prayer teaches us in the same way.

Prayer Manners

The stomach is positioned so closely to the heart that bellyaching affects them both. ;) Though God provides our daily bread, we ought not to view that provision as our right. **"For everything created by God is good, and nothing is to be rejected, if it is received with gratitude; for it is sanctified by means of the word of God and prayer"** (1 Timothy 4:4–5). The word of God in Mark 7:19 makes all foods clean, and gratitude expressed through prayer sanctifies what enters the body for the Lord's service. Just as Jesus gave thanks, be sure to say "please" when you pray.

Reflection Questions

- Who benefits from the act of asking God for what He knows we already need? ____________________

- For what do God (and good parents) wait before supplying the needs of their children?

  ____

- Why is it tempting to grumble and demand from God rather than to ask for His help? ____________________

  ____

- Have you expected blessings from the Lord without humbly asking? If so, how? ____________________

  ____

- Jesus teaches His disciples to request their daily bread, and Paul instructs Timothy to receive it with gratitude. Give one example of God's daily blessing—other than food—for which you ought to give thanks.

  ____

- What small but powerful spoken habit pleases your mother and your heavenly Father? ____________________

  ____

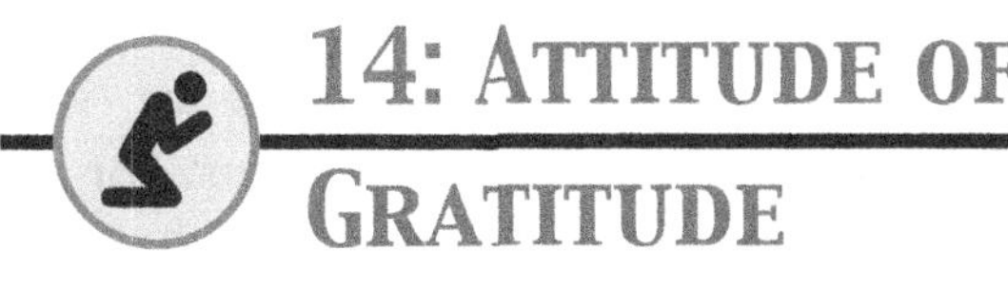

14: Attitude of Gratitude

Please and Thank You

God teaches His children to say "please" so that He may impart to us an appreciation for every good thing and every perfect gift that He provides (James 1:17). God knows what we need, but for our sake He waits to be asked (James 4:2). Today let's consider the other side of that humble coin—gratitude.

These pleasantries make for more than polite prayers. God commands their use. **"Be anxious for nothing, but in everything by prayer and supplication with thanksgiving let your requests be made known to God"** (Philippians 4:6). Or again, **"Devote yourselves to prayer, keeping alert in it with an attitude of thanksgiving"** (Colossians 4:2). Or yet again, **"always giving thanks for all things in the name of our Lord Jesus Christ to God, even the Father"** (Ephesians 5:20). God expects gratitude to accompany our requests in prayer and to be our response to all things.

Honor to Whom Honor

Why is God such a stickler for mannerly prayers? It's worth reflecting on what exactly we're proposing with prayer. Western culture reeks of self-importance, and the odor tends to cling to us even in our prayer closets. How should the Lord be approached? Of second-rate sacrifice Malachi asks, **"'Why not offer it to your governor? Would he be pleased with you? Or would he receive you kindly?' says the LORD of hosts"** (Malachi 1:8). When we pray, is the Lord not due the same honor as a mere public figure?

Our familiarity with the Lord compounded by society's self-conceit can cause us to forget with Whom we speak and Who is ultimately in control. Our prayers should confirm—not erode—our respect for the Lord of hosts (armies). Consider His word, His works, and His nature, and in that context beseech the Almighty and be grateful. **"Let us come before His presence with thanksgiving; let us shout joyfully to Him with psalms. For the LORD is a great God, and a great King above all gods"** (Psalm 95:2–3).

Prayer Manners

Even though the Lord deserves our thanks in all things, we also benefit from the practice of gratitude. To be thankful is to acknowledge God's divine power and position. When we thank God for our daily bread, we confess that He is its provider. When we thank God for health, we recognize the Great Physician as our healer and sustainer. Such acknowledgments produce two distinct benefits. First, they restrain humanity's descent into darkness, for those who would worship the creature must first dismiss the Creator by refusing to give thanks. **"For even though they knew God, they did not honor Him as God, or give thanks; but they became futile in their speculations, and their foolish heart was darkened"** (Romans 1:21).

Second, gratitude has the curious power to transform our trials into blessings, since the perception of our circumstances is often as influential as the circumstances themselves. We usually consider something as bad if it makes us uncomfortable and good if it brings us comfort or pleasure. Unfortunately, this attitude often leads to a misidentification of our lot in life, and we fail to appreciate what God has given us.

If corporate downsizing causes you to lose your job, is it good or bad? Certainly it is uncomfortable. You will have to find a new livelihood and, in the process, perhaps develop greater faith. James refers to that appraisal when he writes, **"Consider it all joy, my brethren, when you encounter various trials"** (James 1:2). The circumstance did not change, but we are admonished to alter our perception of it. That shift happens chiefly through grateful prayer. **"In everything give thanks; for this is God's will for you in Christ Jesus"** (1 Thessalonians 5:18). If I know that the testing of my faith produces endurance, then I can be thankful that the Lord is working to develop that character in me. When we view all things from the perspective of gratitude, we recognize the blessings they could be. Gratitude is a choice.

Father, I thank you that you train me for my good, and I'm grateful that you care enough to grant me the opportunity to learn the lessons I must learn. I recognize my circumstances are Your tools for causing me to grow in faith and character, and I thank you for them. I thank you for the people you've placed in my life who challenge me to become more mature in Christ, and with joy I submit myself to the task.

Reflection Questions

- Philippians, Colossians, and Ephesians all suggest that no prayer is complete without ______________________

  ____

- What might tempt you to neglect—consciously or not—the practice of gratitude in your prayers?

  ____

  ____

- Before their heart was darkened by futile speculations, where did humanity go wrong? ______________________

  ____

- How does gratitude change your perspective on difficult circumstances?

  ____

  ____

- Write three challenges that you face. Before going on to the next lesson, thank God for them and acknowledge that He may use them as blessings in disguise.

  ____

  ____

  ____

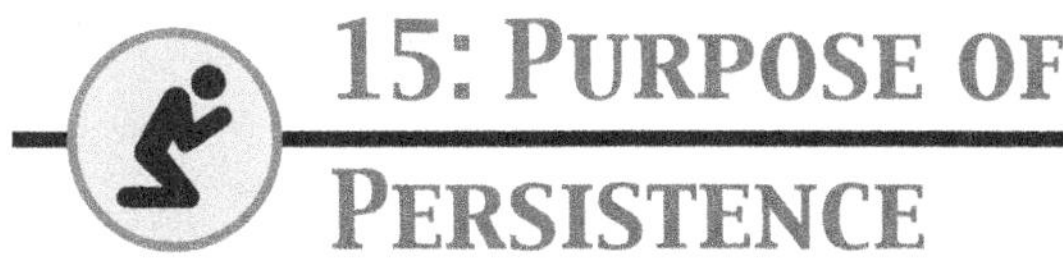

15: Purpose of Persistence

Danger of Discouragement

In our prayers—and our faith in general—we are confronted by an obstacle that would destroy our resolve: discouragement. The mountains we climb in a life of faith are short on glorious vistas and usually marked by mundane footsteps along the trail. We struggle against the impersonal foe of earth's gravity for every foot of elevation gained toward heaven. Beneath the weight of concern and looking to the road ahead, the traveler can lose heart. This seems especially true in prayer. I assume most Christians have often become discouraged in prayer; I certainly have. Hopefully, today's topic will encourage us both. **"Now He was telling them a parable to show that at all times they ought to pray and not to lose heart"** (Luke 18:1).

The parable that Jesus tells is simple. A woman approaches the judge in her city for legal protection, which he is unwilling to grant. Since women do not have legal standing in the culture, he is not obliged to hear her case. This judge is an unscrupulous fellow, fearing neither God nor man, but because of her persistence he finally relents and grants her request. Thus, if a lazy judge can be swayed by the power of persistence, how much more will the Lord act on your behalf? Jesus then asks, **"Shall not God bring about justice for His elect, who cry to Him day and night, and will He delay long over them?"** (Luke 18:7). Take heart and keep praying. God hears and will not long delay.

Bless Me

Jacob encounters a stranger on his return to Canaan, and the two wrestle until dawn is about to break. His opponent dislocates Jacob's thigh, but still the heir of Abraham's promise does not release him. Jacob says, **"I will not let you go unless you bless me"** (Genesis 32:26). An all-night wrestling match and a dislocated hip seem a high price to pay, yet it demonstrates just how highly Jacob values the blessing of God.

Both Jacob (in v. 30) and the stranger (in v. 28) agree that the anonymous opponent that night is the Lord, and this raises several interesting questions for us in regards to prayer. Why would the Lord struggle with Jacob? And if He is able to dislocate his thigh, could He not have ended the contest much sooner?

Persistence and Priority

God wants Jacob to struggle. And He purposely withholds His blessing for that reason. Why? Because what costs us too little, we value too lightly. God isn't trying to keep the blessing from Jacob. The Lord already knows how valuable that blessing is to him, but God wants Jacob to see that for himself.

Persistence proves priority. When my children ask me for something—even something that might be appropriate for them—I may put them off initially. Years ago, one of my boys wanted a pocketknife in the worst way. Now, I would not deny any responsible boy that rite of passage, yet I wanted him to appreciate it. I delayed, but he would not be dissuaded. I placed obstacles in his path, but he demonstrated sufficient responsibility. Finally, he was rewarded.

Persistence, like fasting, demonstrates our faith and communicates the value of our request—to us. Is it not persistence in the Syrophoenician woman that causes Jesus to note, **"O woman, your faith is great; be it done for you as you wish"** (Matthew 15:28). By my count she requests the Lord a minimum of four times while being both ignored and denied. Still her persistence pays and her great faith is rewarded.

The same principle is seen again when Jesus heals the ten lepers. Often the Savior places an obstacle before those bringing their requests to Him, and He does the same with them. Jesus says, **"Go and show yourselves to the priests."** Excuse me? The

Law instructs those who have been cleansed from leprosy to present themselves for priestly inspection before rejoining society, but Jesus gives this command while they are still leprous! Would they persist? "**As they were going, they were cleansed**" (Luke 17:14). Keep praying, and do not lose heart.

Reflection Questions

- If you've been discouraged in prayer, what do you think is the root cause, and how might you address it?

  ____

  ____

- Give two reasons why God might not immediately grant your request. ______________________________

  ____

- Jacob wrestled with God. Why did he struggle all night?

  ____

- Describe the relationship between the cost of our prayers and our appreciation for their answers.

  ____

  ____

- If you measured the importance of your requests by your persistence in prayer, how important would they be?

  ____

- Besides priority, what else does persistence in prayer—or the lack thereof—tell us about ourselves?

  ____

16: Unceasing Prayer

Closet Christians?

There's nothing dazzling about Jesus' instruction, **"But you, when you pray, go into your inner room, and when you have shut your door, pray to your Father who is in secret"** (Matthew 6:6). Today's lesson is frightfully practical. If you were hoping for inspiring insights accompanied by angelic voices, I'm afraid you will be sorely disappointed. Though it's not the most sensational, this topic may well be the most important—consistency.

We have seen how the widow is rewarded for her persistence, and Jesus uses that parable **"to show that at all times they ought to pray and not to lose heart"** (Luke 18:1). Today let's focus our attention on what it means to pray "at all times." The phrase appears with notable frequency. For example, the Thessalonian church is flatly instructed, **"Pray without ceasing"** (1 Thessalonians 5:17). The Ephesians likewise are told, **"With all prayer and petition pray at all times in the Spirit"** (Ephesians 6:18). But what does "at all times" mean?

If you pray at all times, do you pray in both good times and bad? Does sleep count? And if you pray while driving, should you close your eyes? ;)

Consistency

Some have suggested that to "pray at all times" means to leave the conversation unfinished—just blurting out to God whatever comes to mind as it arrives—as if the prayer phone were left off the hook. Others suppose that to pray without ceasing is to make prayer into an attitude that never leaves us, like leaving the prayer switch on.

To pray "at all times" should be defined in the same way as other spiritual directives—by Jesus' example. He is our perfect pattern, therefore, we may test our theory against His practice. Jesus does not remain sequestered in a prayer closet, nor does He seem prone to sudden outbursts of prayer. Jesus does, however, show us an example of consistency: **"But He Himself would often slip away to the wilderness and pray"** (Luke 5:16). We see the same habit in Paul, who always makes mention of the Roman saints in his unceasing prayers (Romans 1:9–10).

In addition to the empirical evidence, comparing Paul's twin letters reveals a helpful connection. Ephesians says, **"Pray at all times"** (6:18), and Colossians echoes, **"Devote yourselves to prayer"** (4:2). (See the graphic on page 28) Thus, to pray at all times means simply to be consistent in the habit of prayer.

Form the Habit

Consistency may be simple, but it ought not for that reason to be confused with ease or insignificance. Notice that both Jesus and Paul make prayer their habit—and priority. Their examples not only define what the Scriptures mean by the phrase "at all times," but they also signify its importance. Jesus prays early in the morning (Mark 1:35) and late at night (Matthew 14:23). The multitudes demand His daylight hours, so the Savior makes time for prayer while others sleep. **"And it was at this time that He went off to the mountain to pray, and He spent the whole night in prayer to God"** (Luke 6:12). I am confident that my daily schedule (and yours) is considerably less demanding than either Jesus' or Paul's, but to pray with their consistency, we must adopt their priority.

Consistency is as important as it is mundane. Habits are not exciting, but small consistent steps are more effective than irregular great effort. Every area of life from physical to financial agrees; the steady tortoise always beats the erratic hare. Even marathons are easy to run a little at a time, and prayer is a marathon. This means we have some choices to make.

Habits (at least good ones) rarely form themselves, and daily tasks are only done at the cost of something else. We must be deliberate, because no one—not even Jesus—prays by accident. If we are to develop the habit of consistent prayer, we must make the appointment. Set a time when prayer is your priority and be willing to lose sleep when the need arises. Only by claiming that time for prayer can we save it from other uses. You'll need a system. Like a training regimen, a track to run on when we pray makes the most of our time. We'll discuss that in more detail later, but consistent prayer will ultimately be effective prayer. Keep praying!

Reflection Questions

- When should a Christian pray? ____________________
- What example defines that kind of prayer? __________
- What does consistent prayer look like?

  ____
- List two comforts that Jesus occasionally went without in order to make time for prayer? ____________________

  ____
- Why is consistent prayer important?

  ____

  ____
- In the last week, how many days have you made time for deliberate prayer? (Meals don't count.) _____________
- When will you deny other claims on your time in order to pray? (Choose a specific time.) _____: ____ a.m./p.m.
- What do you anticipate will be the most significant obstacle to your commitment and how do you plan to overcome it? __________________________________

  ____

17: On Fasting

Christians to Fast

The subject of fasting makes some Christians uneasy if not downright hangry. The practice is usually reserved for the boosting of significant requests, but most often it seems to be awkwardly ignored, marginalized as an antiquated Old Testament practice.

Fasting is not a mystical rite that seizes the attention of the Almighty, but, like other components of successful prayer, it is a rational exercise—proper and understandable.

The disciples of John the Baptist practiced fasting, but Jesus' followers did not. Neither of them pleased the Pharisees and scribes, who disapproved of John and grumbled at Jesus. **"And Jesus said to them, 'You cannot make the attendants of the bridegroom fast while the bridegroom is with them, can you? But the days will come; and when the bridegroom is taken away from them, then they will fast in those days'"** (Luke 5:34–35).

The twelve disciples did not fast when Jesus was with them for two reasons. First, (as He said) it was a time of joy rather than humble penance. After all, the bridegroom had appeared. Second, if they wanted the Lord's attention, all they had to do was ask; He was standing right beside them. However, Jesus did expect the disciples to fast after His departure. To that end, the Lord gave instructions to them and to us. **"But you,"** Jesus said, **"when you fast, anoint your head, and wash your face so that you may not be seen fasting by men, but by your Father who is in secret; and your Father who sees in secret will repay you"** (Matthew 6:17–18).

Heart of Humility

Fasting does cause the Lord to take notice. It is while they are fasting in Antioch that the Lord says, **"Set apart for Me Barnabas and Saul"** (Acts 13:2). Later, Paul and Barnabas also appoint elders with prayer and fasting (Acts 14:23). Even demons are cast out with its influence (Matthew 17:21).

Make no mistake, fasting is no hunger strike to force the Lord into action, but a sign of humility. The great Assyrian city of Nineveh serves as an excellent example. **"And he** [the king] **issued a proclamation and it said, 'In Nineveh by the decree of the king and his nobles: Do not let man, beast, herd, or flock taste a thing. Do not let them eat or drink water. But both man and beast must be covered with sackcloth; and let men call on God earnestly that each may turn from his wicked way and from the violence which is in his hands'"** (Jonah 3:7–8). The wicked city repents at the preaching of Jonah and does so with fasting in sackcloth (another sign of humility). The Lord takes note of their genuine repentance and forestalls their destruction. King David also, when his child is near death, humbles himself with fasting until he receives the Lord's answer (2 Samuel 12:15–23).

Jesus focuses on this aspect when He gives instructions for fasting. **"Whenever you fast, do not put on a gloomy face as the hypocrites do, for they neglect their appearance in order to be seen fasting by men. Truly I say to you, they have their reward in full"** (Matthew 6:16). The idea is to be heard in heaven—not noticed on earth. To use fasting as a badge of pious martyrdom defeats the purpose of humility and does not impress the Lord. Thus, the prayers of the Pharisee in Jesus' parable are not heard despite his meticulous tithing and twice-weekly fasts (Luke 18:10–14).

Fasting Philosophy

One might ask the same question of fasting that we have posed of prayer: if God knows what we need before we ask, why ask? If He hears us when we pray, why pray more than once with persistence? And if the Lord is already willing, what use is there in fasting to gain His favor? It is not God who benefits from our asking, our persistent seeking, or our knocking with fasting. Rather, there is something we must learn from the process.

To put it plainly, fasting shows *us* how much our requests mean to us. A wise father knows that granting some requests should require buy-in from the hopeful child. Before Dad forks over the cash for the new bicycle, he may require Junior to mow some lawns to earn some or all of the purchase price. Similarly, God works with us to teach us the value of spiritual things. Is our request worth more than breakfast? Does our petition rank higher than lunch? Is the answer more important to us than supper? Fasting does not make our request more important to God but reveals how important it is to us—and God notices.

Like unappreciative children who ask for a puppy but are unwilling to demonstrate responsibility or purchase a leash and collar, it's easy for Christians to become dissatisfied with the Lord's provision or the perceived lack thereof. They are disgruntled because they've not received what they wanted, but the Lord would be right as their heavenly Father to ask what they have done to warrant such a gift. If they are unwilling to contribute according to their means, is He wrong to put off their requests?

Ask yourself the question, "How much do my prayers mean to me?" You'll find the answer in your persistence and sacrifice.

Reflection Questions

- What did Jesus anticipate would change about the prayer life of His disciples after He ascended to glory?

  ____

  ____

- To whom should our fast be directed? _______________

- What is the purpose of fasting? ____________________

  ____

- For what important situation have you prayed lately?

  ____

- Is the appropriate resolution of that situation more important to you than lunch? ____________________

- In what two ways can you demonstrate the importance of your prayers? ______________________________

  ____

18: A Proper Fast

Fasting Faux Pas

Jesus says His disciples will fast, but other than some general warnings against doing it to impress my neighbor, the Lord does not give much in the way of instruction; naturally, questions arise. How long is long enough? If my fasting is discovered by others must I start over? Should I fast from food only or from drink as well? And into which category does a fortified smoothie fall? The answer to these gnawing spiritual questions may surprise you. ;)

Daniel is a great example of fasting. After receiving a particularly troubling vision of kingdoms yet to come, the aged advisor of emperors seeks to understand the revelation: **"So I gave my attention to the Lord God to seek Him by prayer and supplications, with fasting, sackcloth, and ashes"** (Daniel 9:3). Again, during the reign of Cyrus the Persian, Daniel fasts for three weeks: **"I did not eat any tasty food, nor did meat or wine enter my mouth, nor did I use any ointment at all, until the entire three weeks were completed"** (Daniel 10:3).

Gnats and Camels

Jesus chides the religious leaders of His day for their preoccupation with relatively insignificant details at the cost of truly important principles, **"You blind guides, who strain out a gnat and swallow a camel!"** (Matthew 23:24). Similarly, we ought not to allow the mode of fasting to outweigh its motive. It's easy to be *consumed* by the details of whether to eat or to abstain, but notice that for twenty-one days Daniel fasts from *tasty* food (meat and wine) and ointment. In essence, the man of high esteem eats bread and drinks water for three weeks. It turns out there is no biblical recipe for a suitable fast in regard to minutia; categories, duration, portion size, and calorie count are left to the individual's judgment. Much like freewill offerings are largely at the discretion of the giver (Deuteronomy 16:10–17), the menu of a fast is up to you. It is not the key ingredient of a proper fast.

Sacrifice of Humility

There is a commonality I cannot help but notice between fasting and the old temple sacrifices. Both speak clearly to the belly, for nearly every offering was edible. Bull, lamb, goat, fowl, grain, wine, or oil—they all went up in smoke reminiscent of a backyard barbecue. God was getting to the heart of man when He required a sacrifice of the stomach.

Let's consider one final example of fasting today. As Esther prepares to go into the king's presence unannounced, she requests, **"Go, assemble all the Jews who are found in Susa, and fast for me; do not eat or drink for three days, night or day. I and my maidens also will fast in the same way"** (Esther 4:16). Certainly this is a critical moment for the Jewish nation, so why not offer a sacrifice at the temple as so many others have done previously? Neither Daniel nor Esther sacrifice to the Lord at the temple because neither could do so. The temple lies in ruins when Daniel needs to entreat the Lord, and though it is being rebuilt in Esther's day, the Persian queen is approximately 850 miles away. When no sacrifice can be offered on the temple altar, God accepts the personal humbling of His people and their offering of fasting.

Fasting is the only sacrifice no one is too poor to offer or too rich to notice.

Reflection Questions

- What is the proper duration of a biblical fast?

  ____

- Are meat, wine, and personal hygiene allowed during a fast? ____

- What matters most in a fast? ____________________

  ____

- What did the ancient temple sacrifices have in common with fasting? __________________________________

- Why didn't Daniel or Esther add a temple sacrifice to their prayers instead of fasting?

  ____

- What is the connection between the stomach and the heart?

  ____

- If you were to fast, what would you surrender in humility to the Lord?

  ____

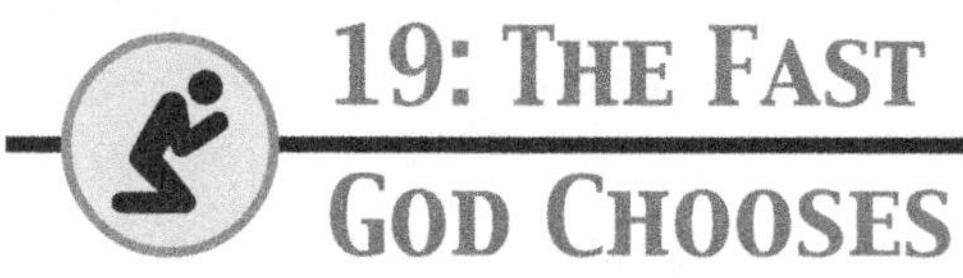

19: The Fast God Chooses

Fast Quarrel

Your stomach will be pleased to know that this lesson is the last on the topic of fasting. ;) Whether New Testament or Old, the practice of surrendering one's daily bread for the sake of the Lord's attention is unchanged, and no passage is so descriptive in this matter as the words of the prophet Isaiah. Through him God spoke to chastise, educate, and motivate regarding fasting, and His words remain relevant today.

It may take several readings of Isaiah 58 before the context and the voice of Isaiah become clear. The speaker alternates from God to the supposed objections of the people and finally to God's response. Take a moment and read the short chapter now. Yes, right now.

The Almighty calls out His people with an indictment of their sins and transgressions. What have they done? They have abused the practice of fasting and their neighbors. But they protest **"as a nation that has done righteousness, and has not forsaken the ordinance of their God"** (Isaiah 58:2).

Contentious Appetite

The people have some accusations of their own. Their fasts are going unnoticed—their humility ignored. **"Why have we fasted and Thou dost not see? Why have we humbled ourselves and Thou dost not notice?"** (Isaiah 58:3). Why doesn't the Lord answer their requests? He counters with His own accusations. The people have not denied themselves any of their desires, and for their fasting workers there is no relief (v. 3). The contention and strife at the heart of their fast is not rectified by the superficial ceremony of bowing with sackcloth and ashes (v. 5).

Even the New Testament agrees, **"You ask and do not receive, because you ask with wrong motives, so that you may spend it on your pleasures"** (James 4:3).

Jesus shows what such contention might look like as fasting becomes a weapon in the hand of His fictitious Pharisee: **"I fast twice a week; I pay tithes of all that I get"** (Luke 18:12). Yet it is not enough to remedy his contempt for his fellow man. The Lord scolds Israel, **"Behold, you fast for contention and strife and to strike with a wicked fist. You do not fast like you do today to make your voice heard on high"** (Isaiah 58:4).

Free the Oppressed

The Lord explains what kind of fasting gets His attention: care for the hungry, the poor, and the naked. **"Is this not the fast which I choose, to loosen the bonds of wickedness, to undo the bands of the yoke, and to let the oppressed go free, and break every yoke? Is it not to divide your bread with the hungry, and bring the homeless poor into the house; when you see the naked, to cover him; and not to hide yourself from your own flesh?"** (Isaiah 58:6–7).

To share your uneaten bread with one who has none accomplishes more than satisfying the hungry. It loosens the hold that sin might have on *you*, that *you* should be free (Isaiah 58:6). Consider how Jesus buffets His body and for forty days makes it His slave by fasting. The flesh is beaten.

Fasting, like our prayers and most aspects of Christianity, is done primarily for the sake of others. David fasts for his enemies (Psalm 35:13). Nehemiah fasts for his people (Nehemiah 1:5). And the church in Antioch fasts for Paul and Silas (Acts 13:3) who in turn fast for the elders they appoint (Acts 14:23). The Lord notices their heart more than their hunger. **"Then your light will break out like the dawn, and your recovery will speedily spring forth; and your righteousness will go before you; the glory of the LORD will be your rear guard. Then you will call, and the**

LORD will answer; you will cry, and He will say, 'Here I am'" (Isaiah 58:8–9).

Reflection Questions

- In Isaiah 58, which verses mark the changes of speaker from God to the people and back to God again?

  ____

- What accusation did the people of Isaiah 58 level against the Lord that might be repeated by modern Christians?

  ____

- According to Isaiah 58:4, how had the people weaponized the practice of fasting? ______________________________

  ____

- Why should they (and we) fast? ______________________________

  ____

- Fasting has a curious liberating effect. From what would you like to be set free? ______________________________

  ____

- How does the Lord respond when a heart of humility practices fasting?

  ____

20: Avoiding Repetition

Well Begun

A desire to know God is the *why* that compels us to pray. Any other motive eventually falls short, and our efforts falter, stutter, and fail. Neither guilt nor greed, neither duty nor public honor can produce a lasting relationship with God any more than they can yield a successful marriage. A short-term relationship might be possible, but in those motives are the seeds of its destruction. Compulsory prayer will get a person no closer to God than the Law will bring him or her to righteousness.

However, let's turn our attention today to the *how* of prayer. I approach this topic with some reluctance because it is not our aim to all pray alike. My hope is to consider the substance common to us all and to leave the style to you.

People naturally tend to pray in the way they think they should. You may use Bible vocabulary and Christian-isms to make your prayers more polished, formal, and—dare I say—holy, but formality can also lead to a kind of detached dishonesty. If you're frustrated with your neighbor or even with God, tell Him. Do so respectfully, but avoid the mistake of communicating only the things that sound pious and good. If you have doubts that challenge your faith, tell Him. If you find sin attractive and your efforts to overcome are failing, tell God what you're really going through and how you feel. Remember He was made like you in all things, was tempted just like you, and can sympathize with your weakness (Hebrews 2:17–18, 4:15). The Lord knows what it's really like to be in your shoes. Praying what we think God wants to hear is not true conversation.

As a dad, I want my children to share their lives with me. I am not offended when they honestly relate their struggles, frustrations, or even their failures. I don't want them to edit their conversations to impress me at the cost of honest relationship.

More than anything, I want to know their hearts. When you pray, share with God as you would encourage your children to share with you since you care for them: **"Casting all your anxiety upon Him, because He cares for you"** (1 Peter 5:7). Tell Him. He understands.

No More Blah, Blah

Jesus gave His disciples some prayer instruction that is easier said than not said: **"And when you are praying, do not use meaningless repetition, as the Gentiles do, for they suppose that they will be heard for their many words"** (Matthew 6:7). It is human nature for the mind to follow familiar patterns, develop habits, and generally fall into a rut. This is true enough in prayer, where that rut can easily degenerate into meaningless repetition. When our children were younger, their nightly prayers were often the same. "Thank you for dad, mom, brothers, sisters, pets, et cetera." Imitation and practice had produced a homogenized mantra in Jesus' name, amen. It was a start.

To keep the mind out of that rut, add different terrain to the conversation. The late Don DeWelt of Ozark Christian College promoted the idea of praying from the Scriptures. His booklet, *Sweet Hour of Prayer,* and its companion, *Personal Worship,* are worth reading, and I am indebted to him for this key concept.

When we pray from the Scriptures, they become the framework to which our thoughts are attached. Like a tune beneath the lyrics, the Word of God structures our personal praises and requests. It is easier to demonstrate than to describe. Let's use Psalm 25 as the foundation for praising God; go ahead and read along. If I use David's inspired sentiments as the basis of my own, I might pray:

> "My Lord, to You alone do I lift up my soul, for I know You care for me. In You, my God, I can place all my trust. You are ever faithful. Men may fail, but though the whole world be found a liar, You are proven right. Father, You see those who

would shame me and exult over me, for nothing escapes Your notice..."

In this way every line reveals something more about God's character. Who knew that God was concerned with shaming the treacherous and preserving those who wait for Him?

Using the Scriptures as the basis for our prayers is not without biblical precedent. Nehemiah is a Jewish official in the Persian Empire who is well acquainted with the Scriptures. When he learns of the dismal state of Jerusalem, the cup bearer to the king seeks the Lord's help using the Scriptures as the basis of his request. His prayer to God on behalf of his people begins with a quotation from the prophet Daniel: **"I beseech Thee, O LORD God of heaven, the great and awesome God, who preserves the covenant and lovingkindness for those who love Him and keep His commandments"** (Nehemiah 1:5 and Daniel 9:4).

Nehemiah humbles himself and reminds the Lord of His previous promise to Moses. In Nehemiah 1:8 he again quotes the Scriptures, this time borrowing from Leviticus 26:33: "**Remember the word which Thou didst command Thy servant Moses, saying, 'If you are unfaithful I will scatter you among the peoples.'"**

In the New Testament also, the early Church lifts its voice to God using the inspired lyrics of the Psalms. They begin their prayer (recorded in Acts 4:24–26) by addressing God as the One **"Who made heaven and earth, the sea and all that is in them; Who keeps faith forever"** (Psalm 146:6), and they praise Him in the voice of David: **"Why are the nations in an uproar, and the peoples devising a vain thing? The kings of the earth take their stand, and the rulers take counsel together against the LORD and against His Anointed"** (Psalm 2:1–2).

The Scriptures are an inexhaustible source of insight into the nature of God, and, praying from them, you'll never find yourself in the rut of meaningless repetition. The Psalms especially are ready made for this purpose since they themselves are inspired prayers. But take care. The Word of God is not a magical book of spells for recitation to effect the changes we desire or to manipulate God into action. This is not another Jabez's prayer. The Scriptures are, however, the words of the Lord Himself, and to speak His words is to think His thoughts. We are, as Paul describes, **"combining spiritual thoughts with spiritual words"** (1 Corinthians 2:13). When our thoughts are aligned with those of the Lord, and we speak back to Him through them, that is the basis for real conversation—the goal of our time spent in prayer.

Imaginary Friend

A final thought: God is certainly not imaginary, but it's easy for people to imagine their relationship with Him based on what they think God should be like. Praying from the Scriptures guards against this tendency of speaking to an imaginary (and therefore usually agreeable) friend. We need to be constantly reminded of who God is from His Word lest we begin to remember Him more conveniently. Only the Scriptures keep our perception of God grounded in reality. Prayer from the Scriptures may seem awkward at first, but it soon becomes easier. It's worth it. Keep praying!

Reflection Questions

- Why do short-term motives fail to produce a lasting relationship with God? Be specific.

  ____

- What problem can arise from attempting to pray "correctly?" ________________________________

  ____

- What primary quality can make the content of your prayers meaningful? __________________________

- Match the feeling on the left with the appropriate action on the right.

___ Joy	A. See a therapist
___ Sorrow/Shame	B. Tell God
___ Boredom	C. Use King James English
___ Anger/Frustration	D. Write a book on prayer ;)
___ Anxiety	

- What practice appears often in Biblical prayers and helps us avoid the bog of meaningless repetition and the fantasy of subconscious projection?

  ____

  ____

21: Formats and Elements

A Pattern

Experienced instruction is invaluable to newbies. The learning curve is much more manageable if we can observe and imitate. Whether playing the trumpet or driving a car, some simple pointers and a example to follow make all the difference. Today let's learn a pattern for prayer.

Some elements ought to be included in our prayers. Jesus' template in Matthew 6 includes a recognition of four components: God's position, will, provision, and forgiveness. Mnemonic devices have been suggested to help Christians remember and incorporate those prayerful ingredients. One such reminder is the acronym ACTS: Adoration, Confession, Thanksgiving, and Supplication. The idea is to pray from the Scriptures (as we discussed previously) with a view to adoring God, confessing sin, thanking God, and finally making our requests. In this way most of the major elements of prayer are covered, and the pattern gives the inexperienced a track to run on. I think such guides can be useful, especially when initially developing the habit of prayer. They help us maintain some structure. But remember—motives come before mechanics.

If you're having trouble with setting some direction for your conversation with the Lord, ACTS is a good place to start. We'll consider each of these elements (Adoration, Confession, Thanksgiving, and Supplication) in more detail, beginning today with praise.

Faucets of Praise

The bulk of our prayers really consists of praise to God; even earthly kings are approached with praise. The pandering peasants of Acts 12:22 employ the undue praise of flattery, but even Paul recognizes Agrippa as the king, an expert in all customs and questions among the Jews—and presumably a patient listener (Acts 26:2–3). The apostle is simply showing honor to whom honor is due. How much more ought we to honor the Lord with appropriate praise? **"Enter His gates with thanksgiving, and His courts with praise. Give thanks to Him; bless His name. For the LORD is good; His lovingkindness is everlasting, and His faithfulness to all generations"** (Psalm 100:4–5).

Immediately some readers will have conjured images of compulsory praise. How many times can you say, "Holy, holy, holy," before it becomes meaningless repetition? But this is not at all what it means to praise God. Praise (for our purpose) is much the same as a wife who finds that her husband has fixed the leaking faucet. She recognizes his character through the action and praises him accordingly. *"I noticed the faucet has stopped leaking. Thanks, you're such a handy fella."* Our praise, too, is the organic result when we notice the Lord's character and acknowledge it back to Him. It is perhaps the primary way we come to know and appreciate our Heavenly Husband.

When reading the Scriptures, our minds must be trained to seek out and notice the praiseworthy. With that mindset, almost all of the Bible becomes a window into the character of God seen through His words and actions. Try this exercise: using Psalm 11, find one of God's traits from each of the seven verses and acknowledge them back to Him. Praise Him for being your refuge as if He were a mountain to which you might fly. You might be surprised at what you learn.

Volume Preference

Does God prefer spoken prayers or silent ones? A person who cannot speak is not hindered from addressing the Lord. Paul sometimes lapses into prayer in the middle of his epistles, so written prayers are fine too. What are psalms, after all, but written prayers? Some have suggested that to pray effectively we really ought to write our prayers, but that's bogus. The mode of prayer is irrelevant to God. There can be value in keeping a prayer journal—a logbook of dates, requests, scriptures used, et cetera, but there's nothing pious about paper. Use the mode that best facilitates undistracted conversation with God. Our goal is relationship—not this many pages filled or that many scriptures read.

After trying them all, my personal preference is spoken prayer. My mind is far too busy to be productive with my eyes closed in silent communion with God. Perhaps that speaks ill of my piety, but the truth is that when I speak only in my mind it takes minutes (if not seconds), and I'll be distracted or asleep.

Written prayer is also personally frustrating because I tend to become preoccupied with handwriting or typing speed. It also takes too long. Audibly spoken prayer works wonderfully for me. It uses the tongue to steer the mind and keeps up with the speed of thought. Try them all, but use whatever method works best for you.

Reflection Questions

- What is the best way to learn how to pray?

- List the four categories of prayer found in Matthew 6.

- From Psalm 11 and in your own words, list one characteristic of God and the text that identifies it.

- Using the characteristic you identified, write out a simple prayer that includes adoration, confession, thanksgiving, and supplication.

22: A Confession to Make

Clean Conscience

When Jesus teaches His disciples to pray, His example includes this request: **"And forgive us our debts, as we also have forgiven our debtors"** (Matthew 6:12). The Lord anticipates the need for forgiveness and therefore for confession, but it is not His aim to make them the foundation of our relationship with Him. God removes the guilty conscience from the Christian so that we might have fellowship with Him based not on guilt but on the love that produces genuine worship. To that end, Christ's effectual sacrifice has cleansed His people so that they **"would no longer have had consciousness of sins"** (Hebrews 10:2).

This is not to say we should be unaware of sin—far from it. The child of God is all the more sensitive to his shortcomings, but with his conscience cleansed (Hebrews 9:14), the saint, like Paul, should be able to say, **"For I am conscious of nothing against myself"** (1 Corinthians 4:4).

Sadly, many Christians believe their position in Christ is in constant jeopardy. They assume that if they sin, their fellowship with Christ is broken until such time as they have offered the appropriate sacrifice in the form of penance, prayer, or confession. This is wrong.

New Testament grace is a radical departure from the Old. Under the first covenant, forgiveness was reactive. If you did the crime, you paid the fine in the form of sacrifice. However, in Christ, grace is now proactive. Hebrews beautifully describes the single sacrifice of Christ in contrast to the continual offerings for sin demanded by the Law. **"But He, having offered one sacrifice for sins for all time, sat down at the right hand of God"** (Hebrews 10:12). One sacrifice implies there will be no more, and the Scriptures agree. **"Now where there is forgiveness of these things, there is no longer any offering for sin"** (Hebrews

10:18). The one offering of Christ has permanently replaced any sacrifice that might have been offered by the temple priests then or any that you or I might offer now as the penalty for sin. That is to say, your sins—past, present, and even in the future—have already been forgiven. Let that sink in for a minute.

A relationship based on guilt and sacrifice already existed under the Law. If our prayers have replaced compulsory temple attendance, and the sacrifices of confession are a modern reminder of sin, we have truly devalued the cross.

> *If you are unsure whether you have received the proactive grace available through Jesus under the New Covenant, please see the appendix at the back of this book.*

Two Bad Options

The opposite error is no better. To ignore sin is also to marginalize the sacrifice of Christ, for those who would abuse His mercy have insulted the Spirit of grace (Hebrews 10:29). Thus, as with so many scriptural principles, we find that to err on either side is to turn to law or conversely to lawlessness.

Marriage again is an invaluable illustration. What if every conversation with your spouse began with prerequisite guilt, confession, and forgiveness? *"Hi Sweetheart! How was your day? Did you live up to all of your marriage vows? Is there any way you fell short of my expectations? Was there more you should have done to please me?"* That's not communication; it's grounds for divorce! ;) Even so, many Christians believe they must begin their prayers with humble contrition to be heard.

Those precious moments together as husband and wife must sometimes be about honesty and apology, but that should not be the focus of our time spent with God. Where is the balance that deals effectively with sin yet gently with the sinner?

Confident Grace

The throne of our High Priest is one of grace, not guilt or condemnation. **"Let us therefore draw near with confidence to the throne of grace, that we may receive mercy and may find grace to help in time of need"** (Hebrews 4:16). Grace allows us to be completely honest with God without fear of punishment, for, **"If we confess our sins, He is faithful and righteous to forgive us our sins and to cleanse us from all unrighteousness"** (1 John 1:9).

God desires—no, demands—that we remain honest in our dealings with Him because **"Those who worship Him,"** Jesus says, **"must worship in spirit and in truth"** (John 4:24). Sin itself is not the principle issue—honesty is. Christians live in grace, and if one should sin the Lord does not take it into account (Romans 4:8). But hidden sin is a different matter. **"If we say that we have no sin, we are deceiving ourselves, and the truth is not in us"** (1 John 1:8).

We know if we have broken faith with the Lord. Likewise, if I sin against my wife by gambling away our paycheck, I have some explaining to do, and an honest (and difficult) conversation is appropriate. Spouses ought not to punish each other for their honesty, but to work together to find solutions to their shared problems. So it is in our relationship with the Lord. There may be situations that require an honest and difficult conversation about our failures, and that is the topic of our next lesson.

Reflection Questions

- Why isn't confession the primary component of New Testament prayer?

  ____

- How does New Covenant grace differ from Old Covenant grace? ____

  ____

- What "sacrifice" could you offer as settlement for your sin?

  ____

- Does grace mean that you can ignore sin? Why or why not? ____

  ____

- According to Hebrews 4:16, how should you come to God even if you have sinned? _________________________

  ____

- Why is God more concerned with honesty than with sin?

  ____

  ____

23: Confession in Practice

Sacrifice of Confession?

Today's tender topic of confession is the second element in the A-C-T-S of prayer, and I'm confident it will change the way you pray. In every relationship there are points of friction—areas where we or they did not live up to the expectations of the other. In our relationship with Christ, we sometimes find that we have also failed to meet His expectations. This is called sin. It must be dealt with, as in any relationship, through repentance and confession. And though it is a necessary part of our divine marriage, it is not the central element. As we discussed previously, in Christ our conscience is—and must remain—clean.

Sin & Guilt

Many view confession as the New Covenant equivalent of Old Covenant sacrifice. They believe that forgiveness of sin is conditional on appropriate repentance demonstrated through the sacrifice of their confession of sin. They believe that once the offering of confession has been presented, they are restored to grace and fellowship until another sacrifice should be required. 1 John is sometimes cited in support of this belief, but a careful reading of the passage reveals this is misguided.

"If we confess our sins, He is faithful and righteous to forgive us our sins and to cleanse us from all unrighteousness" (1 John 1:9). It certainly sounds as if confession is the key that opens God's grace to the penitent. But how can this be if—as we discussed in lesson 21—grace is proactive? If that is true, then sin has *already been forgiven*. What are we missing?

The primary issue in this passage is not sin. Instead, honesty is John's focus and must be ours as well. An honest person confesses and receives forgiveness in contrast to the dishonest person described in the alternating verses who lies and does not practice the truth (v. 6, 8, 10). Notice that John is describing two two personified strategies for dealing with sin—honest and not so much.

The same issue is explored in David's wonderful psalm of grace, confession, and forgiveness: **"I acknowledged my sin to Thee, and my iniquity I did not hide; I said, 'I will confess my transgressions to the LORD'; and Thou didst forgive the guilt of my sin"** (Psalm 32:5). This is nearly a perfect reflection of 1 John 1:9, but the context provides a hidden gem. Notice that the sin that David acknowledges in verse 5 is forgiven in verses 1-2: **"How blessed is he whose transgression is forgiven, whose sin is covered! How blessed is the man to whom the LORD does not impute iniquity, and in whose spirit there is no deceit!"** Apparently, not only have sins of the past been resolved, but God does not impute (attribute) sins of the present! But why, if the price for sin has already been paid, should David confess it? He answers that question by identifying what has been forgiven: guilt. "**And Thou didst forgive the guilt of my sin"** (Psalm 32:5). We note with joy that the relationship of grace described by David applies to us since Romans 4:7-8 quotes the very same verses to describe those who are righteous apart from works—that means you.

The Mosaic Law included separate sacrifices for guilt and sin (Ezekiel 40:39, and the two are dealt with separately in marriage as well. Forgiveness is the business of the one wronged, but guilt is the burden of the offender. Though no restitution may be necessary, guilt remains until the problem is confessed, dealt with, and resolved.

Christ-Focused Confession

God demands honesty in our prayers—especially in confession. Thus the well-meaning saint, eager to confess and put guilt behind him or her, tackles the problem head on.

> Lord, forgive me for being such an unrepentant miserable wretch. I knew it was wrong to (your sin here), but I was tempted, and the more I thought about _________, the more I wanted _________, and that made me think about _________ some more, and finally I did _________ because I'm a loser.

This might be honest, but it is not profitable. Paul warns that devotion to the Law allows sin to provoke a desire for the very temptation we're trying to avoid: **"But sin, taking opportunity through the commandment, produced in me coveting of every kind; for apart from the Law sin is dead"** (Romans 7:8). When the children of God must confess, how might they do so honestly without mentally dragging themselves through the mire again—as in the previous example—focusing on the very thing they do not wish to do?

Should confession be required of you again, try the following. I have used Psalm 33:4–5 for demonstration purposes, but any passage that highlights the character of God will do. Follow along in the psalm, and it will be easy to see how those words can become your own for the purpose of confession.

> My Lord, Your word is upright; indeed, You cannot lie. Even Your work is done in faithfulness, fulfilling Your promises, true to Your word. Righteousness and justice are a delight to You and to me, and the earth shows Your lovingkindness throughout. Your sun and rain fall on all men alike. Father, I must apologize for (your sin here). I did not live up to Your standard of uprightness. Forgive me for not being faithful in all my work just as You are. You have caused me to become your righteousness through

Christ; help me to live in a way that better reflects Christ in me. I am so grateful for Your kindness; it knows no bounds. Help me show it to others also.

If we confess sin as a deficiency in our appropriation of Christ's character (which it is) we are free to deal with the transgression honestly and still keep our focus where it belongs—on Christ rather than on the details of our failure. If this sounds unconventional, consider David's famous confession recorded in Psalm 51. Take note of how the king honestly expresses his sin and his anguish because of it without rehashing the gory details of his indiscretion. He sets his eyes on the goodness of God. Keep praying.

Reflection Questions

- How does confession differ from sacrifice? ______________

____

- Describe the two characters in 1 John 1. Which one has committed sin? What is the difference between them?

____

____

- What do you learn about sin and confession from 1 John 1:9 and Psalm 32:5? ______________________________

____

- What do Psalm 32:2 and Romans 4 say about how God assigns our potential future sins? ____________________

____

- What aspect of sin can only be resolved by confession?

____

- Why shouldn't you focus your prayers on sin?

____

- What would be a more profitable focus when confession is necessary? ______________________________________

24: Importance of Thanksgiving

Habit of Thanks

After the topic of confession we have lots to be thankful for, and that will be the focus of our discussion as we consider the T in the A-C-T-S of prayer. In lesson 13, "The Attitude of Gratitude," we considered the larger principle of thanksgiving. Today we will discuss its nuts and bolts in our daily prayers.

Colossians 3:17 encourages, **"Whatever you do in word or deed, do all in the name of the Lord Jesus, giving thanks through Him to God the Father."** All is to be done by the authority of Christ accompanied by the giving of thanks. Gratitude, like other virtues, is more than action. It is the result of deliberate choices molded by habit and cemented into character. Thankful prayer focuses our attention on the good even when it's difficult to find. Over time the practice of **"always giving thanks for all things in the name of our Lord Jesus Christ to God, even the Father"** (Ephesians 5:20) becomes the habit of seeing circumstances and people for their potential, as God does, and being truly thankful.

Getting Personal

Thanksgiving can be as general or as specific as you'd like. It's easy to find reasons to be appreciative on a large scale. One might thank God as the author of creation or redemption. Or one might meditate on the level of detail that brings a specific character trait of Christ into focus and be grateful, for example, for the way Jesus demonstrates tireless compassion toward the multitudes. Perhaps most acute is our appreciation expressed for what the Lord has done for us personally. It's one thing to praise and thank God for who He is and what He has done for all mankind, but it's something else to consider what He means to me and what He has done on my behalf.

The general grace of God shows His love for all of Adam's fallen descendants, but His grace toward each of us individually makes that grace personal: **"And He Himself is the propitiation for our sins; and not for ours only, but also for those of the whole world"** (1 John 2:2). The forgiveness of the whole world demonstrates the love of God, but His forgiveness toward me shows that He loves me.

That kind of personal gratitude also changes our relationship. When we are deliberate about thanking God for all things—even difficult things—our personal circumstances take on new meaning. Now joys, challenges, and even trials are potential blessings from the Lord; they become gifts from God rather than random obstacles. Our appreciation for the Giver follows. It changes our hearts when we choose to see God's love in our lives through gratitude. Hint: it works in marriage also. ;)

Gratitude Sample

As usual we want to use the Scriptures as the basis for our prayers. When it comes to giving thanks, the Word of God is replete with examples. Having trouble getting started? Psalm 107 will give you weeks of material. We'll use v. 1 and 2.

> My Lord, I owe You a debt of thanks. In You I live, and move, and exist, for you formed me—body, soul, and spirit. There is no one good but You. You cause the rain and sun to fall on the righteous and unrighteous alike, but You have been so gracious to me. Your kindness is everlasting. How could I begin to remember all of Your kindnesses? Even so, they pale in comparison with what You have accomplished for me in spirit. I cannot thank You enough that You have caused my soul to be redeemed from the hand of the devil. I am ever grateful.

Reflection Questions

- Describe the stages of adopting gratitude as part of your character. In which one are you?

  ____

  ____

- How can you be thankful for your circumstances, both good and bad? ______________________________

  ____

- How might your gratitude change from the thirty-thousand-foot view to the ground level of life?

  ____

  ____

- Jesus said, "Where your treasure is, there will your heart be also" (Matthew 6:21). How can you apply this idea to prayer with gratitude?

  ____

  ____

- List three items, one general, one specific, and one personal, for which you are grateful to God.

  ____

  ____

25: List of Favors

Change of Will

The requests that Jesus mentions in His template prayer have little resemblance to the laundry list of favors that are sometimes forwarded to the Almighty. The S in A-C-T-S stands for supplication, and today let's consider just how our requests should be made known to God.

Jesus makes requests respectively for the coming of the Lord's kingdom, His will, daily bread, forgiveness, and deliverance from evil (Matthew 6:9–13). We have previously considered which requests the Lord answers and how to ascertain God's will in our circumstances (see lessons 6, 10, and 11). Today, our attention turns to what that looks like in the daily practice of our requests.

Though both are involved, prayer is less about changing God's will into our own than it is about conforming our will to His. Notice the balance that Jesus strikes between His desires and those of the Father. The majority of His requests are for the Lord's sake rather than for His own. A similar pattern is observed in the prayers recorded throughout the Scriptures. The requests of the sender are considered against the greater backdrop of the receiver.

His Will

In many cases we do not know God's will, especially as it applies to the specifics of our situation. Such questions as where to go, which job to take, whom to marry, and do I want fries with that, must be evaluated on the basis of the principles in the Scriptures and the wisdom of the individual. Even though we might not always know how to pray as we ought, we can still petition the Father on behalf of His will.

Jesus said simply, **"Thy will be done"** (Matthew 6:10). He practiced submission to God's will daily; thus it's no surprise that we see it surface in His most strenuous hour in the garden (Matthew 26:42). Submission to God's will in the little things makes submission in the big things possible, and we can pray as Jesus did.

Sometimes the will of God is quite clear. The spread of the gospel, the personal growth of the saint, and the love of the brethren are prayers we may send with full confidence that they are congruent with God's will. They have been solicited "in His name;" that is to say, they are in step with the authority of Christ as delegated to us, His ambassadors (2 Corinthians 5:18–20).

Practice of Requests

God wants to hear our prayers, and He invites us to make our requests, **"casting all your anxiety upon Him, because He cares for you"** (1 Peter 5:7). From a practical standpoint, how should this be done? There are many things that warrant our attention and are "prayer worthy," but to list them all each day is cumbersome and repetitive, often leading to mechanical recitation.

Conversely, it's easy to overlook items that ought to be included in our prayers. My solution for both problems is a written list divided into seven categories corresponding to each day of the week. This division allows me to pray each day for a manageable number of folks, congregations, and situations far and wide, and the list ensures that nothing is left out over the course of the week. My wife and I had six children just so that my prayers would work out evenly. ;) Actually, that wasn't the reason, but it's handy that I can pray for Jen on Sunday and each of the kids on a certain day of the week, seven people for seven days. A different solution may be more suitable for you, but this is my simple answer to the problem.

Whatever your requests, set them in the language of God's Word. The following is a heavily redacted and generalized sample of what my requests might sound like on any given Lord's Day if Psalm 89:1–2 were the text:

> My Lord, Your lovingkindness deserves endless praise. You have made Your faithfulness known to all generations, unchanging, built up forever like the heavens. May Your throne be exalted by this generation also as sharers in Your covenant with Christ. Father, please watch over the saints scattered abroad, especially those in Colorado and Florida. Please consider the needs of two families in Missoula and one dear saint in Spokane. I am grateful for the gift of Your kindness in my wife, and I pray on her behalf. Please use the Inner Man Radio project to promote your faithfulness, and use me in the Bible studies scheduled for today to share Your lovingkindness.

Reflection Questions

- Does prayer change our will to be consistent with God's, or does it change His will to be consistent with ours?

  Explain. ______________________________________

  ____

- What is one "little" area in which you ought to submit your will to God? ______________________________________

  ____

- When will you start? ______________________________

- Why should we pray, "Thy will be done"?

  ____

  ____

- Make a list of requests (for people, events, situations, et cetera) and schedule a day to pray for them on the table on the following page. Feel free to make something that better reflects your personal situation. The table provided is just to get you started.

Daily Prayers

	Sun	*Mon*	*Tue*	*Wed*	*Thu*	*Fri*	*Sat*
Family							
Church							
The Lost							
Bible Studies							
My Needs							
Other							

26: Three Options to Pray

Laps—Not Lapse—of Prayer

Some of you free spirits are growing tired of this systematic approach to prayer, and so today will be the last discussion about the mechanics of that most-personal time with the Lord. It is not at all my intention to numb your mind with laps of prayer—around and around and around—but, personally, I go farther with a track to run on than without. With that in mind, today let's consider three tracks and two examples. But, as with all running, consistency is key. Our goal is not to find the perfect system, but to use a system to build consistency.

All elements of prayer can be roughly divided into the four basic categories we've discussed: adoration, confession, thanks, and requests. Our task is to accomplish these through the use of the Scriptures themselves. So, your time with the Lord should begin by selecting a passage to pray from. Three to five verses is usually sufficient for me to find qualities of God from which to praise, make confession, give thanks, and present my requests. For example, when I prayed through Psalm 16, I split the passage into three manageable pieces. I used the first four verses on day one, verses five through seven the next day, and finally verses eight through eleven. Psalm 17 began the day after and so on.

Three Tracks

We have already discussed the first and simplest of our tracks: A-C-T-S (Adoration, Confession, Thanksgiving, and Supplication). The second track worth considering was developed by the late Don Dewelt and is explained in detail in his pamphlet "How to Establish and Maintain Your Personal Worship." In it, Dewelt expands the four primary prayer categories into twelve steps for personal devotions. They are:

1. Praise *for* God;
2. Praise *to* God;
3. Confession;
4. Sing a prayer;
5. Read His Word to Him;
6. Read His Word for yourself;
7. Read His Word in thanksgiving;
8. Read His Word in meditation;
9. Read His Word for daily petitions;
10. Listen;
11. Intercession;
12. Sing a prayer of praise.

This track may seem a bit rigid at first to spontaneous hearts, but the process leaves very few stones unturned and is worth your consideration and experimentation. Though it is not my personal preference, Dewelt's approach forces us to look for things we would see otherwise. Try it, but find what works for you.

The third option for our purpose today—and my personal choice—is simply to categorize the elements of Jesus' pattern prayer of Matthew 6:9–13. By my reckoning, the Lord's Prayer can be distilled into the praise and recognition of God in these six subdivisions: God's position, God's will, God's provision, God's forgiveness, God's deliverance, and God's authority. Praying through each of those using the qualities of God as seen through your selected scripture for the day will illuminate who God is in ways you've not considered before and make your daily prayer time fresh and meaningful. Try each of them, or a combination thereof, but plan to pray.

Private Prayers

Sadly, not many of Jesus' prayers are recorded for us. Apparently He follows His own advice (Matthew 6:6) and prays in private: **"But He Himself would often slip away to the wilderness and pray"** (Luke 5:16). Paul, likewise, prays often, even sometimes as he writes to the churches far and wide (Romans 15:13). But the personal prayers of the apostle are not preserved for us.

The best examples of personal prayer are those of David and the other psalmists. Those prayers to music address the Lord on every topic. Praise, thanks, confession, and request are all on display as directed by the inspiration of the Holy Spirit. The psalms are not a rigid framework or formula for prayer, but they serve as examples of the attitudes and subject matter appropriate to the exercise. They deal with every area of human emotion: resisting temptation; confession; fear; gratitude; and praise, praise, praise. Use them.

I suppose it's human nature to look for the easy way. Whether it's a fitness routine, a new diet, or living within your means, there's always a new wonder supplement or life hack that offers all the benefits without any of the work. Such novelties come and go, but the real magic isn't in the plan. The most important element in any good habit—and especially in prayer—is consistency. You simply cannot succeed without it no matter what cool new gimmick you use.

Don't quit; it's about to get really good.

Reflection Questions

- Why is it valuable to experiment with different systems of prayer if you're a free spirit at heart? ____________________

  ____

- What is the advantage of using a prayer system?

  ____

- Select 3–5 verses from The Psalms and write the reference below. Most any will do, but your chosen verses should highlight the nature of God.

  ____

- Choose one of the tracks of prayer to use today and circle it:

  A-C-T-S, the Dewelt 12, the Lord's prayer

- Right now, pray using the track and passage you selected together with your request schedule from the previous lesson.

- What facet of God's character did you notice that you hadn't seen that way before?

  ____

- What word best describes your prayer time today?

  ____

27: Obstacles to Prayer

My Neighbor

I wish I could tell you that, after learning how to pray using the Scriptures (the topic of the last several lessons), you will easily maintain the habit. If that were true, it would have been the first topic in this series instead of nearer the end. In truth, there are obstacles to prayer that we must confront if we are to be successful.

One such obstacle is your neighbor. I do not mean that your neighbor restrains you from praying through his faults, threats, or coercion, but your attitude toward him can. God limits our relationship with our heavenly Father on the basis of our earthly neighbor (1 John 4:20). Take note. Your relationship with God can go no farther than the relationship with your neighbor.

Brother and Father

Jesus teaches His disciples, **"If therefore you are presenting your offering at the altar, and there remember that your brother has something against you, leave your offering there before the altar, and go your way; first be reconciled to your brother, and then come and present your offering"** (Matthew 5:23–24). Simply put, before our relationship with God can move forward, we must deal with the relationship with our neighbor.

This may seem odd, but consider that our love of the brethren is the real test for our love of God. **"Whoever loves the Father loves the child born of Him"** (1 John 5:1). Therefore, whoever claims to love God and simultaneously hates his brother is a liar (1 John 4:20) . A child cannot harm a brother or sister and expect the relationship with his or her father to be unaffected. Yet, Christians sometimes forget they must love their siblings in Christ if they are to have any relationship with their mutual Father. For this reason husbands are admonished to treat their wives—who are their sisters in Christ—with the honor due **"a fellow heir of the grace of life, so that your prayers may not be hindered"** (1 Peter 3:7).

Forgiveness

How do I make my brother or sister in Christ behave? If they would straighten up, I could love them as children of God, and my prayers would not be hindered. Alas, friend, you give too much power to your neighbor. We may not cede control of our relationship with the Lord to someone else.

My attitude toward my neighbor is my decision and under my control. I have the power to forgive him unilaterally without his repentance or penance on the basis of the grace extended to me. Like the slave forgiven much in Jesus' parable, I have the right and responsibility to extend the forgiveness I have received from the Lord to my fellow servant (Matthew 18:21–35). If this were not so, and I could not forgive until those who had wronged me sought my forgiveness, I could not pray as Jesus advised, **"forgive us our debts, as we also have forgiven our debtors"** (Matthew 6:12).

More than that, I am empowered to request the Lord on their behalf. **"If anyone sees his brother committing a sin not leading to death, he shall ask and God will for him give life to those who commit sin not leading to death"** (1 John 5:16). It's difficult to hold a grudge against someone while at the same time asking the Lord to forgive him. In this way prayer for our neighbor changes us more than him. Your pesky neighbor may continue in his foolishness, but your attitude toward him will be changed by the exercise of seeing him through the Lord's eyes in prayer. By diligently loving our neighbor in prayer, we find God's door open to us.

Reflection Questions

- How does a person's relationship with others affect his or her relationship with God? ______________________________

____

- According to Matthew 5:23–24, which relationship must be restored first before the other can be made right?

____

- Do you suppose wives are required, like husbands, to treat their spouses with honor if their prayers are to be heard unhindered? _________ Why or why not? _______________

____

- Who has the unilateral authority to forgive? ______________
- How much forgiveness does Matthew 6:12 say you will receive? ____________________________________

- What effect does prayer for my neighbor (especially the obnoxious type) have on him or her? ________________

____

- What effect does it have on me? ______________________

____

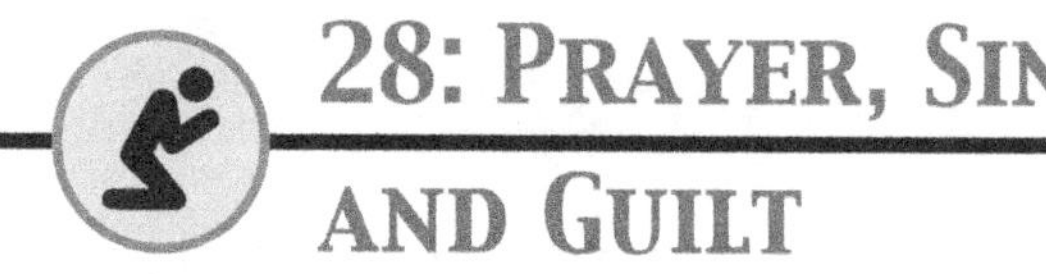

28: Prayer, Sin, and Guilt

Sin and Death

The harmful effects of sin just cannot be overstated. By its very nature sin is self-destructive. It corrupts the body and the mind, entangles the careless, and enslaves those who practice it. Like cancer of the soul, sin infects and seizes control of that which is good, twisting it into an agent of death. Even the Law and commandments are not immune to its corrosive influence: **"For sin, taking opportunity through the commandment, deceived me, and through it killed me. So then, the Law is holy, and the commandment is holy and righteous and good"** (Romans 7:11–12). Sin uses even the Ten Commandments to deceive and ultimately to kill, revealing its inherent evil, **"that through the commandment sin might become utterly sinful"** (Romans 7:13).

The spoiling influence of sin is no less potent when it comes to prayer, and it is perhaps the greatest obstacle to developing a meaningful and consistent habit. **"But your iniquities have made a separation between you and your God, and your sins have hidden His face from you, so that He does not hear"** (Isaiah 59:2). The prophet Isaiah scolds a people who **"draw near with their words and honor Me with their lip service, but they remove their hearts far from Me, and their reverence for Me consists of tradition learned by rote"** (Isaiah 29:13). Sadly, the people of Isaiah's day are not very different from their modern counterparts. Their prayers have become mechanical obligations devoid of any true relationship with their God who no longer listens to their sin-calloused hearts. **"We know that God does not hear sinners; but if anyone is God-fearing, and does His will, He hears him"** (John 9:31).

Christians enjoy the tremendous blessing that their sins have been covered and are remembered no more. But if a child of God chooses to continue living in sin, the terror of impending judgment will ultimately replace the confidence of Christ's sacrifice (Hebrews 10:26–27).

We cannot really maintain a relationship with the Lord in the presence of sin. If you are unsure that your sins have truly been forgiven, please see the appendix on salvation at the back of this book.

Conscience

Christians are emboldened to pray because our High Priest sympathizes with the weak and deals gently with the misguided (Hebrews 4:15–5:2). When he finds his sinful self in the presence of God, Isaiah cries out, **"Woe is me, for I am ruined! Because I am a man of unclean lips"** (Isaiah 6:5). But unlike the prophet, a Christian's clean conscience welcomes him or her to the throne of grace. **"Beloved,"** says John, **"if our heart does not condemn us, we have confidence before God"** (1 John 3:21).

Conversely, a guilty conscience is repelled at the thought of honesty with God: **"For everyone who does evil hates the light, and does not come to the light, lest his deeds should be exposed"** (John 3:20). Nothing separates a person from God like guilt. Since the day God walked the garden in search of Adam and Eve, humans have been hiding from God, ashamed of their condition, and there is a great temptation for Christians to do likewise.

The sin-guilt-avoidance cycle bears an uncanny resemblance to the process of divorce. It generally goes like this. If we sin we have immediate guilt in the knowledge of what we have done. Guilt is uncomfortable, and avoidance is an easier path than dealing with it directly in prayer. In our personal lives it may look like skipping prayer time, but it restarts the cycle because after a couple days away from the Lord in prayer, we now have another issue to feel guilty about. Now we must explain to God not only the original sin problem but also our growing distance. The additional guilt makes it that much more difficult to be honest with the Lord. Further avoidance seems an easy solution, and the feedback cycle continues. Each recurrence gradually hardens the heart until separation is the result. We give up on prayer altogether and find ourselves like Israel in Isaiah's day, just going through the motions of relationship with God. If this describes you, take courage.

Start

Prayer is immensely powerful and is the only way to break the cycle of sin, guilt, and separation. We will discuss why this is so over the last two lessons, but for our purpose today remember this: it is impossible over the long term to have a meaningful relationship with God through prayer and continue in sin. Conversely, it is impossible to continue in sin and have a meaningful relationship with the Lord. No one can serve two masters; one or the other must emerge the victor. The master you serve is the one that wins.

If sin has kept you from the habit of prayer, you must realize two things. First, the Lord is a faithful, merciful, and sympathetic high priest ready to welcome you. Second, there will never be a better time to break that cycle than right now. Right now, recognize that you have no secrets from the Lord, and silence about the facts does not change them. Right now, understand that the longer you put off prayer, the harder it will be to come back to it. Right now, stop allowing sin to keep you from conversation with God. Right now, not later today—*right now*—this very moment, before you leave your seat and before you put down this book, open the conversation with God. I'll get you started:

> Heavenly Father,
>
> There is nothing You do not know. You know my efforts to do right and my failures. You know my desire to maintain a relationship with You and the obstacles I face…
>
> but I choose You…

Reflection Questions

- What do you learn about sin from Romans 7:11–12?

  ____

- How does sin affect prayer from your perspective and God's? ______________________________________

  ____

- What do you learn about the cycle of sin from the story of Adam and Eve? ________________________________

  ____

  ____

- How does sin affect marriage? How does it affect your relationship with God? __________________________

  ____

- Why is meaningful prayer incompatible with sin?

  ____

- Which one will prevail in your life? ____________

- Did you start today? _______ Why, or why not? (Be honest.) ____________________________________

  ____

29: Agent of Change

Failed Attempts

Today's discussion begins the last and (I hope) most encouraging topic on the subject of prayer—prayer as a means of changing character and ultimately our behavior. Many earnest though misguided souls attempt to effect heart-level change through external agents. Such attempts are doomed to failure. Some look to remorse as a talisman to ward off temptation. "If I am sorry enough," they think to themselves, "I will not reoffend." Many tears and much self-abasement follow, but fleshly indulgence remains.

Accountability promises better results. The shame of confessing to another surely outweighs the passing pleasure of sin. Alas, this is no improvement. Since he or she is only accountable when in the presence of a confessor, the one confessing is more likely to seek shelter in hypocrisy or deceit than to pass on sinful pleasures.

In desperation the ignorant look to the familiar grit of good old-fashioned self-control to curb fleshly desires. However, the force of will imposed on the appetites of immorality, impurity, sensuality, et cetera only strengthens such desires, ensuring failure when the flesh is weak and opportunity knocks. Though appearing wise, none of these strategies can change the heart.

"If you have died with Christ to the elementary principles of the world, why, as if you were living in the world, do you submit yourself to decrees, such as, 'Do not handle, do not taste, do not touch!' (which all refer to things destined to perish with the using)—in accordance with the commandments and teachings of men? These are matters which have, to be sure, the appearance of wisdom in self-made religion and self-abasement and severe treatment of the body, but are of no value against

fleshly indulgence" (Colossians 2:20–23). External efforts fail to produce a change within, since the appetite for sin remains.

No matter how genuine their intentions or how diligent their efforts, those who depend on the commandment or self-inflicted consequence to effect change will meet the same fate as those who labored beneath the Old Testament Law since they have merely replaced one tablet with another. Sacrifices of bulls and goats could never reach the heart; their superficial cleansing of the flesh never penetrated the soul or cleansed the conscience.

"For if the blood of goats and bulls and the ashes of a heifer sprinkling those who have been defiled, sanctify for the cleansing of the flesh, how much more will the blood of Christ, who through the eternal Spirit offered Himself without blemish to God, cleanse your conscience from dead works to serve the living God?" (Hebrews 9:13–14).

Glorious Change

Good news! There is a way to transform the inner man so that his external words and deeds become clean also. **"But we all, with unveiled face beholding as in a mirror the glory of the Lord, are being transformed into the same image from glory to glory, just as from the Lord, the Spirit"** (2 Corinthians 3:18). Paul compares the ministry of Christ with that of Moses, who had the singular honor to see God atop Mount Sinai. Though only a glimpse of the Almighty's back was allowed the Law-giver, nevertheless it proved miraculous. Unbeknownst to Moses, his appearance had been altered and he shone like the sun. He had been transformed by the glory he witnessed into the image of that same glory (Exodus 33:18–34:35).

As extraordinary as that transformation was, the Scriptures assert that the New Covenant (to which you and I belong) far surpasses Moses' experience. **"For if the ministry of condemnation** [the Law] **has glory, much more does the ministry of righteousness** [the New Covenant] **abound in glory"** (2 Corinthians 3:9). Like Moses, we too behold the Lord's glory—

though we see Him through the mirror of the Scriptures—and our inner man is transformed into the image of His radiant character.

Speaking with Him

This seems a long way from our topic. What can Moses' experience on Mount Horeb possibly have to do with my prayers? Everything. When we say that Moses saw God, that is certainly true. And when we say that the sight caused Moses to be changed, that also is true. However, a careful reading of Exodus identifies something else as the cause of Moses' miraculous transformation: **"And it came about when Moses was coming down from Mount Sinai... that the skin of his face shone *because of his speaking with Him*."** Later, when the tabernacle was in use, **"whenever Moses went in before the LORD *to speak with Him*, he would take off the veil until he came out.... So Moses would replace the veil over his face until he went in *to speak with Him*"** (Exodus 34:29, 34–35, emphasis added).

Seeing God—and the resulting transformation—takes place at the same time as speaking with God. Now read the above excerpt again, paying close attention to the role that speaking with God plays in Moses' transformation. The implications for prayer could not be more profound.

Through prayer we see and speak with God face to face. Through prayer we behold His glory, and there, unveiled before Him, we are transformed into His image. Pray, and be transformed.

Reflection Questions

- What are the three approaches often used to avoid sin that do not produce lasting results? ________________

____

____

- Why don't external efforts stop us from sinning?

____

- What do you learn about inner transformation from 2 Corinthians 3:18? __________________________________

____

____

- Moses was changed by God's glory. What was he doing when he saw God? ________________________________

- What miracle happens to you when you pray from the Scriptures and look intently at God's character?

____

- Describe one change in yourself since you began to pray using the Scriptures to see God more clearly.

____

30: Seeing and Speaking

Visions of God

When Moses ascended Sinai, he was afforded a rare privilege indeed. Some, such as Ezekiel and Isaiah, saw God by revelation; others looked at God through assorted veils—the burning bush, the pillar of cloud and fire that led the Israelites through the wilderness, or the human form that spoke with Abraham in the heat of the day (Genesis 18:1) but concealed the full glory of Yahweh. Few have been exposed to the glory of God, for He Himself said, **"You cannot see My face, for no man can see Me and live!"** (Exodus 33:20).

Moses was therefore shielded from the full force of that glory in the shelter of the rock and covered by the Lord's hand. **"Then the LORD said, 'Behold, there is a place by Me, and you shall stand there on the rock; and it will come about, while My glory is passing by, that I will put you in the cleft of the rock and cover you with My hand until I have passed by. Then I will take My hand away and you shall see My back, but My face shall not be seen'"** (Exodus 33:21–23).

The sight of God by whatever means He chose to reveal Himself certainly affected those who saw Him, but they did more than see the Lord. As we discussed previously, they spoke with Him and were transformed.

Unveiled Glory

There is no clearer vision of God's glory than Jesus, whom the Scriptures describe as **"the radiance of His glory and the exact representation of His nature"** (Hebrews 1:3). Or again, **"And the Word became flesh, and dwelt among us, and we beheld His glory, glory as of the only begotten from the Father, full of grace and truth"** (John 1:14).

The glory of God is the nature or character of the Almighty, **"who alone possesses immortality and dwells in unapproachable light"** (1 Timothy 6:16). His glory often appears as that unapproachable light, but veiled in flesh it shines through Jesus of Nazareth. Many saw Jesus the man, but at first only a few recognized Him as the Son of God, which is to say, God in the flesh. It was not His appearance, but His character that they recognized as divine.

Having acknowledged Jesus as the Lord of glory, the Son of God, and the King of Kings, how do we then look upon Him? No artist's rendering has preserved the face of Jesus for us. But even if we did know what His physical appearance looked like, flesh and blood would not reveal His nature.

Remember when Peter answers the Lord's question of identity? In one of his shining moments, the chief apostle acknowledges, **"Thou art the Christ, the Son of the living God"** (Matthew 16:16). How has Peter drawn such a remarkable conclusion? It is not Jesus' external appearance that reveals His nobility, for He Himself says, **"Flesh and blood did not reveal this to you"** (Matthew 16:17). Rather it is what Peter has observed of Jesus' character shining through His words and deeds that reveals Him to be the Son of God.

To effect the miraculous change we discussed in the previous lesson, the child of God must "see" Christ. That is to say, he or she must recognize who Jesus is. How? Staring at a lifeless portrait will not acquaint you with its subject any more than stalking someone online will make you friends—that's creepy. Similarly, simply knowing *about* Jesus does not make Jesus know you—conversation (prayer) does.

Open Eyes

When we pray, "Our Father who is in Heaven," we direct the eyes of our hearts upward. Then, using the Scriptures as the basis for our prayers, we find ourselves face to face with the very character of God. We praise Him for who He is, confessing if necessary our shortfalls in light of His unveiled nature. Our gratitude for His love and kindness and even our requests based in His Word remind us of the God to whom we speak, and we set our spiritual eyes upon Him.

When we pray, our primary goal is not the items we request or even the forgiveness of guilt that comes through confession. When we go into our inner room and shut the door and pray to our Father in secret (Matthew 6:6), our principal motive is to know the Lord. For when we pray it is then that we ask, like Moses, "Show me Your glory." And God reveals Himself to us.

Reflection Questions

- Describe what the Bible means by the glory of God.

  ____

  ____

- What did Peter "see" about Jesus that flesh and blood did not reveal? ______________________________

  ____

- How did he see it? ______________________________

  ____

- How can you actually know someone? ______________

  ____

- What do we see when we pray? ______________

  ____

- How has this lesson changed your motive for prayer?

  ____

  ____

31: WORTH THE CLIMB

God's Intent

From the beginning, God has pursued fellowship with humanity. Despite our troublesome fleshly nature (Romans 8:7–8), the Lord has been diligent in His attempts to live with us. He begins with Adam and Eve walking in the garden in the cool of the day (Genesis 3:8). Seven generations after Adam, Enoch is also described as walking with God just as Noah and Abraham would later (Genesis 5:24, 6:9, 24:40). The tabernacle and its successor, the temple, likewise are God's physical attempts at cohabitation, though humanity proved unwilling. The New Covenant provides a means to put the fleshly nature and guilt aside and walk in newness of life (Romans 6:4), and God's desire can finally be realized, for we walk by the Spirit (Galatians 5:25).

Prayer is the central element of that fellowship with God. As Jesus prepares His disciples for His imminent departure, He speaks to them about the Helper He would be for them and about their relationship with the Father. Of prayer He says, **"Until now you have asked for nothing in My name; ask, and you will receive, that your joy may be made full"** (John 16:24).

Jesus is making the hand-off. He wants the disciples to have their own relationship with the Father. Jesus would not ask the Father for them after His resurrection; instead, they could speak with Him directly, **"for the Father Himself loves you"** (John 16:26–27). The joy of that relationship for us and for Him is found in prayer.

Up the Mountain

I cannot make you pray, and even if I could it would be of no benefit. Prayer—like all relationships—is ruined by the promise of reward or threat of punishment. You will only pray if you *choose* to have a relationship with God.

Seeing God face to face through prayer can be uncomfortable because it makes us face ourselves in His presence. It takes effort, and some are unwilling to make the sacrifice. However, others want—no, need—to see God.

Jesus **"took along Peter and John and James, and went up to the mountain to pray"** (Luke 9:28). There atop the mountain, they see Jesus as they have never seen Him before. The simple clothes of the man from Nazareth are replaced with robes as bright as light. Even His face is altered and shines like the sun. Peter, James, and John have trudged up the mountain to accompany Jesus as He prays, but what they see is the picture of glory.

Likewise, prayer transforms us when we behold the Lord through our praise, gratitude, confession, and requests. Even Jesus was not immune to its affects. He was visibly transformed in the same way that we are changed spiritually when we behold the character of God in prayer.

Why do you suppose only those three disciples go with Jesus up the mountain? It appears to be evening, for they are overcome with sleep. Perhaps the nine remaining disciples choose to catch a few winks instead of joining Jesus. And, then of course, there is the mountain. Perhaps the effort necessary to drag themselves up the slope with Jesus at that late hour is just more than they are willing to give. Whatever the reason, I wonder if Jesus doesn't invite all the disciples, but only those three are willing to accept His offer.

Jesus invites all of us to meet Him atop the mountain of prayer, to see Him as He is, to speak with Him face to face, and to be transformed. There will always be trivial matters that complicate the task, but that is true of any relationship. Who will go with Him? Who wants to see God?

Your relationship with God is worth the climb.

Reflection Questions

- Despite the considerable setbacks, what has been God's goal for humanity since the beginning?

  ____

- What makes a relationship with God possible?

  ____

  ____

- Write the verse from John 16 that reveals Jesus' reason for confidence that the disciples' prayers (and yours) will be heard by God. ______________________________

- Why does God want to hear your prayers?

  ____

- What happened to Jesus when He went up the mountain to pray? ______________________________

  ____

- If Jesus invited you to pray with Him, would you climb the mountain? ________ Why? ______________________________

  ____

- Review your answers from lesson one, and give yourself a new letter grade. ________

Appendix

How to Know You're a Christian

Have I truly become a Christian? No question is more important, and none, it seems, has more varied answers. Every denomination, sect, and religion has its own formula—many of which are contradictory. Which one, if any, is right?

Salvation is not a denominational issue. There is not one gospel for Catholics and another for Protestants, mystics, Jews, or atheists. How can we be sure we've been born again, our sins forgiven, and that the Holy Spirit dwells in us?

Only the Bible can answer that question. Our salvation is not determined by our own certainty, consensus, or how many Sundays we've dozed off in Church. ;) The Bible alone must form the foundation of our faith and confidence. There is only one way to God, for Jesus said, **"I am the way, and the truth, and the life; no one comes to the Father, but through Me"** (John 14:6).

The Scriptures outline several steps of faith that everyone passes on their way to becoming a Christian. Like stairs, every subsequent step is based on the foundation of the one before. These steps are not arbitrary; they are central to the Christian life. Thus, until a person is willing to take that step to become a Christian, he or she is not yet ready to live as one.

Step One

FAITH IN JESUS AS LORD

This is as foundational as it gets, but it's where every disciple must begin. A generic belief that Jesus lived or some vague recognition that He is in Heaven is not what the Bible means when it talks about faith in Jesus. Biblical faith is the conviction that Jesus is Lord. Faith recognizes Him as king—THE King! That is the message Peter first preaches on the Day of Pentecost: **"Therefore let all the house of Israel know for certain that God has made Him both Lord and Christ—this Jesus whom you crucified"** (Acts 2:36). And it is the message Paul later preaches to the Gentiles in Philippi when the jailer asks, **"Sirs, what must I do to be saved?"**. Paul and Silas answer, **"Believe in the Lord Jesus, and you shall be saved, you and your household"** (Acts 16:30–31). Notice that in both cases the disciples must believe the truth of Jesus as *Lord* in order to be saved.

Step Two

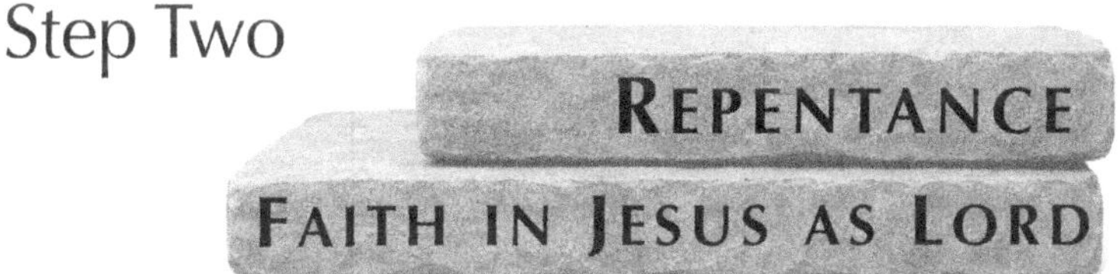

When people come to faith in Jesus as Lord, they recognize their accountability toward God and begin to think differently about their behavior. Their faith produces a resolve to turn away from sin and brings them to step two—repentance.

Our word *repent* is translated from a Greek word that means *change your thinking*. Such a change is required for forgiveness. Jesus says, **"And that repentance for forgiveness of sins should be proclaimed in His name to all the nations, beginning from Jerusalem"** (Luke 24:47), and that is precisely what happens in Acts 3. The good news of salvation is proclaimed in conjunction with repentance: **"Repent therefore and return, that your sins may be wiped away, in order that times of refreshing may come from the presence of the Lord"** (Acts 3:19).

In order for sins to be wiped away, repentance must come first. But it doesn't stop there. Living as a Christian involves continually allowing the Lord to change your thinking so that you act in a way that pleases God. If someone is willing to repent to become a Christian, only then is he or she ready to live as one.

Step Three

CONFESSION
REPENTANCE
FAITH IN JESUS AS LORD

When people hear the word *confession*, they tend to think of sin, and sometimes the Bible uses the term in that way. However, in regard to salvation, another kind of acknowledgment is necessary—the confession that Jesus is Lord.

This public admission is the outward expression of what Paul calls the "word of faith." It is the result of belief, not a substitute for it. The apostle continues, **"If you confess with your mouth Jesus as Lord, and believe in your heart that God raised Him from the dead, you shall be saved; for with the heart man believes, resulting in righteousness, and with the mouth he confesses, resulting in salvation"** (Romans 10:9–10). But why should salvation require confession? Because that's what Christians do.

If you're planning to be a Christian in private, never sharing your faith and remaining silent, you're not yet ready to live as one. Jesus tells the disciples, **"Everyone therefore who shall confess Me before men, I will also confess him before My Father who is in heaven. But whoever shall deny Me before men, I will also deny him before My Father who is in heaven"** (Matthew 10:32–33). If we want Jesus to claim us publicly, we must be willing to do the same.

Step Four

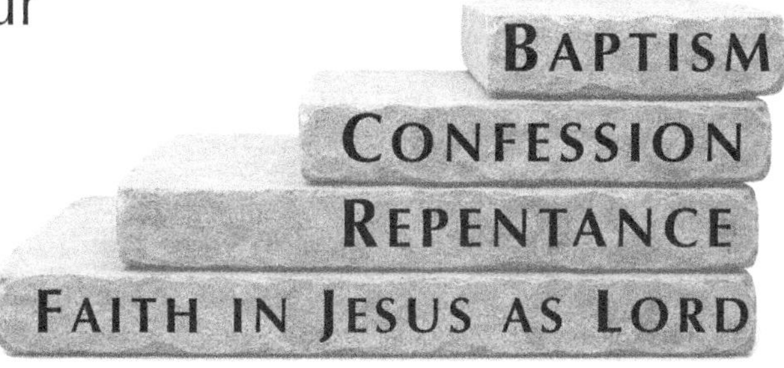

There are several types of baptism in the New Testament, but only one in reference to salvation—the baptism in Jesus' name. Name denotes authority; thus baptism *in His name* is an extension of that foundational faith in Jesus as Lord. **"And Peter said to them, 'Repent, and let each of you be baptized in the name of Jesus Christ for the forgiveness of your sins; and you shall receive the gift of the Holy Spirit'"** (Acts 2:38). Peter is clear; baptism results in forgiveness and is the means through which one receives the Holy Spirit.

The baptism by Jesus' authority/in His name occurs in water. **"'Surely no one can refuse the water for these to be baptized who have received the Holy Spirit just as we did, can he?' And he ordered them to be baptized in the name of Jesus Christ"** (Acts 10:47–48).

There's nothing special about the water. Faith—not water—is what makes the actions of repentance, confession, and baptism effective. **"And Philip said, 'If you believe with all your heart, you may.' And he answered and said, 'I believe that Jesus Christ is the Son of God.' And he ordered the chariot to stop; and they both went down into the water, Philip as well as the eunuch; and he baptized him"** (Acts 8:37–38). Belief produces baptism.

Baptism is not a sacrifice to pay our debt of sin. It is not a work by which we save ourselves any more than repentance or confession make the cross redundant. Baptism is an appeal. It is the way we request salvation by faith in the authority of Jesus as Savior. **"And corresponding to that, baptism now saves you—not the removal of dirt from the flesh, but an appeal to God for a**

good conscience—through the resurrection of Jesus Christ, who is at the right hand of God" (1 Peter 3:21–22).

Peter makes it clear that though water is involved, the mere washing of the flesh is not the active ingredient. Faith is what makes baptism effective as an appeal to God. Thus, if someone were immersed without understanding (faith) in its two-fold purpose of forgiveness of sin and receiving the indwelling presence of the Holy Spirit, he or she has not really been baptized at all—they've been "bath-tized." ;)

Why baptism? It symbolizes on the outside what happens where you cannot see. **"Or do you not know that all of us who have been baptized into Christ Jesus have been baptized into His death? Therefore we have been buried with Him through baptism into death, in order that as Christ was raised from the dead through the glory of the Father, so we too might walk in newness of life"** (Romans 6:3–4). In baptism the body is buried in and raised from water, but more importantly the old self of sin is crucified and buried and the new self raised with Christ (Romans 6:1–11).

Like the other elements of salvation, baptism is an integral part of the Christian life. When God's people share their faith, they must also share how to act on it; it's what Christians do. If someone is willing to be immersed to become a Christian, he or she is ready to shoulder the responsibility of helping others do the same.

Much more could be said about the steps of faith, but our purpose here is simply to outline the Biblical process of conversion—not to elaborate on every facet of the process or address every possible objection. If you have already become a Christian, give thanks to God for His great mercy and resolve to live as one. If you haven't, please consider God's offer of a clean conscience and life through Jesus. If you're unsure, don't put off a confident relationship with Christ and live with uncertainty. Find the answer to this question: have I truly become a Christian? If you need help on that journey, use the email provided.

— Mark mark@innermanpress.org

Made in the USA
Coppell, TX
18 February 2026

71779110R00080